Academic Libraries and Research:

Mastering the Maze
2nd Edition

KENDALL/HUNT PUBLISHING COMPANY
4050 Westmark Drive   Dubuque, Iowa 52002

Book planning, design and publication coordination by Kathleen Weessies.

Copyright © 1996, 1997 by Kendall/Hunt Publishing Company

ISBN 0-7872-3732-9

Printed in the United States of America
10 9 8 7 6 5 4 3 2 1

CONTENTS

iv

vi

Preface

Learning does not cease when one completes a degree program and graduates from college. For many people, real knowledge will be acquired daily through life's experiences. In most fields of endeavor, the knowledge and skills necessary to perform well are never completed. We have all become life-long learners.

At this point in time in society has been nicknamed the "Information Age." We expect that formal education will not only impart factual information to students but will teach them to question, analyze, and critically evaluate all information that is presented to them. The skills that are needed for this critical thinking and analysis are important to every individual who wishes to become an educated person.

This text is intended to assist the college student in learning how to learn. Its purpose is to acquaint you with the myriad of information resources available and to enable you to know how to ask the right questions when seeking information. It is not essential for a student to learn the titles of hundreds of information resources. Rather you must hone certain "detective" skills in order to determine what you need to know.

This book is not a textbook for those in the field of Library and Information Science. It is designed to be used by any student in his first year of college. Like the textbook designed for the course which orients a student to college life in general, this text is intended to acquaint the beginning college student with the kinds of information resources in an academic library and with information resources available through other means. By learning the skills necessary to be information literate, any student can be equipped to meet the demands of the future.

Introduction

Regardless of the major area of study that a person chooses to undertake while attending a college or university, and regardless of whether or not he or she desires to be the best in that particular field, a student will eventually pass through the portals of the campus library. The time taken by the student to conduct research in the library is not wasted, provided students have some knowledge about how to effectively and efficiently find and use the materials located there.

Information is a commodity that everyone needs during some part of his life. College students especially need it to complete projects and assignments for classes. Students will not stop needing information after they have graduated from college. In many cases that is where the need for information really begins. It is a part of one's every day life and, yet, it is still something for which they have little skills or formal training. Many students are not aware of the materials available to help them complete papers or presentations. To become skilled at research, university libraries offer several opportunities for students to become oriented to the layout of the library and the resources located there. Programmed texts, computer-assisted instruction programs, audiocassette tours and videos are all worthwhile mechanisms for achieving these goals. However, the best way for students to learn the layout of the university library and to become skilled at using the various sources located there is to take a structured class — credit or non-credit.

The authors understand that all libraries are not created equal. College and university libraries range from small collections with little electronic access, to the very large institutions that have nearly every conceivable resource available. The library may be housed in one building or be a collection of buildings across the campus. Regardless, they have one major commonality — the frustrated student who is trying to locate information to complete research for a class project. This textbook is designed for use in any academic library setting.

This textbook was written to offer students a way to learn the basic general resources available, as well as those falling into three broad subject categories — humanities, sciences and social sciences. When used as a guide for locating general information, it will help in any course offered in the curriculum. It is also a manual for use in locating information in one of three subject-specific fields. This textbook is not an end in itself. It is to be used with accompanying materials — written, verbal and electronic — to provide a good foundation on which to build.

The authors have designed the course and this textbook from the knowledge they have acquired from teaching and working with students for many years in a variety of secondary, academic and special libraries. They recognize that different students respond better to different methods of teaching and have designed the class to accommodate a variety of teaching styles. They also recognize that students "learn by doing" and have incorporated assignments into the class that provide students with opportunities to gather and organize information into a usable product. Students also will be able to evaluate the information they have located, applying several criteria.

Chapters 1 and 2 offer a brief historical synopsis of library materials and libraries development and a breakdown of the research process for writing a term paper. Chapter 3 gives an overview of classification systems and the various catalogs, with particular emphasis placed on the online catalog found in academic institutions. Chapters 4, 5, and 6 introduce the user to paper indexes, electronic indexes, and general reference tools. Chapters 7 and 8 are dedicated to government publications and the Internet. These first eight chapters are written as general introductory material for any undergraduate student. The remaining four chapters discuss subject-specific research, with individual chapters presenting resources in the broad subject areas of humanities, sciences and social sciences. They are intended to cater to the needs of students who have decided on a major in one of these areas.

The exercises are designed to be a teaching tool, as well as a graded part of the course. When each class moves into the second phase pertaining to one of the three broad subject areas, other exercises will be offered which are not in this textbook. One will consist of evaluation of paper and electronic sources dealing with a specific topic, and another project will include the formatting of citations according to a specific style manual.

The research course for which this text is written is intended to be taught in two phases — general and subject-specific. The first part of the class will be devised so that any college student will benefit from it, while the second part of the class will concentrate on one (and only one) of three subject areas — humanities, sciences or social sciences. This does not mean that a student who has not decided upon a major area of study will not benefit from being in a section dedicated to one of these subjects. ON THE CONTRARY, the way that the subject-specific part of the course is taught can be transferred to any of the other two broad subjects. For example, any student in one of the sections dedicated to the sciences who then decides to major in business will have the groundwork to transfer the knowledge acquired concerning the sciences over to the social sciences. It is believed that once a student has mastered one subject area the research skills will be transferrable to other areas.

1 THE DEVELOPMENT OF LIBRARY MATERIALS AND LIBRARIES

Library materials had their beginnings when early civilizations began to collect ideas and thoughts in written formats. Written materials could not exist until man had the ability to communicate through a system of writing. It is impossible to establish when the first person made crude marks on an object--marks that would eventually lead to a written language. Those early attempts at writing were known as pictographic writing or picture writing, because picture symbols were used to represent an object (Vervliet, p. 18). Later a number of those symbols were combined to create simple ideas. Eventually each symbol was represented by a sound rather than an object or idea. Once that occurred any word within spoken language could be written (Olmert, p. 30). Historians generally agree that written history began about five thousand years ago. Prior to the advent of a written language, ideas and thoughts were communicated through the spoken language. Many early writings came from those spoken traditions (Marshall, p. 20).

Mesopotamia

Western civilization had its beginnings in an area known as the Fertile Crescent, the area that extends from Egypt along the eastern shore of the Mediterranean Sea to the Persian Gulf. This area, known as Mesopotamia, was one of the most active areas of early civilization. Mesopotamia translates as "the land between the rivers." Located to the north of the Persian Gulf, Mesopotamia surrounded the river valleys of the Tigris and Euphrates rivers.

Cuneiform was the standard form of writing and clay tablets were the standard material which people of Mesopotamia used for their written communications and records (Vervliet, p. 20). Those who could read and write in Mesopotamia were the religious leaders and some of the political leaders. General collections of written materials into what might be called libraries were of interest to the religious and political leaders. The typical library collection would contain important religious writings, census data on people and property (generally for tax purposes), and official government correspondence, both internal and external.

Among the more important written works of the area of Mesopotamia was the Code of Hammurabi. The Code is important because it was the beginnings of written legal codes. King Hammurabi had the code inscribed upon pillars of stone throughout the kingdom. Although most people could not read the code, they were reassured by its existence. They had more faith that the laws were stable and not subject to constant change. Within western traditions the Code of Hammurabi and a shorter legal code known as the Ten Commandments used by Moses and the Jewish nation became a basis for law that is reflected within modern jurisprudence. Both of those legal codes led to written interpretations which were hundreds and thousands of times more lengthy. Thus to an extent those two early legal codes led to the creation of law libraries (Harris, p. 9).

Egypt

The location of the Nile river valley isolated the Egyptian civilization from others. That isolation allowed Egypt to develop a unique culture (Avrin, p. 81). The Egyptian leaders inscribed records about their society on stone walls, many of which have survived the ravages of time. As was the case in Mesopotamia, the major collections of written materials in Egypt were for religious and governmental reasons. In fact the two were often the same, since Pharaoh often claimed to be a god. About 1250 B.C. a major Egyptian library existed in Thebes. Rameses II took pride in this library which contained over 20,000 scrolls (Gates, p. 10).

The written language of the religious and political leaders of Egypt is known as hieroglyphics. The word is the combination of two Greek words which mean sacred carvings or religious writings (Olmert, p. 31). The natural resource for writing materials for Egyptians was papyrus, a reed which grew wild along the Nile river (Avrin, p. 82). Papyrus was made into scrolls. The Rosetta Stone gave the world the key to the long-forgotten language of ancient Egypt. A French officer of Napoleon's engineering corps discovered it in 1799 (Olmert, p. 32). It gave the same inscription in two languages and three alphabets, including hieroglyphics. Comparing the translation of a known language revealed the meaning of the hieroglyphics. The Rosetta Stone was later taken to England, where it is still preserved in the British Museum (Avrin, p. 42).

The Development of Early Alphabets

About 1500 B.C., an ancient Semitic alphabet was developed (Avrin, p. 17). The Phoenicians, who lived along the eastern shore of the Mediterranean Sea have generally been given credit for spreading the use of an alphabetical system (Gates, p. 9). The Phoenician alphabet contained twenty-two signs and was developed around 1100 B.C. The Greek and Roman alphabets contain elements of the widely distributed alphabet of the Phoenicians.

Libraries of the Greeks and Romans

It was not until the time of Plato, Aristotle, and their students that the Greek world was to make an important impact upon the written literary world. The fifth century B.C. was the golden age of

> ## THINK ABOUT THIS....
>
> Today, some people compare the way the federal government is beginning to offer information to the public with the way public libraries in ancient Rome offered information for the upper class, with no regard for the common man. This divides the public into two groups: the "haves" and the "have nots." Since the federal government is offering more and more information in electronic format these days and doing away with print, those with the ability to view the information will have an advantage over those who cannot afford to buy the necessary equipment to view it. True, the information will be available in public libraries, but some say that the federal government is giving the advantage to those who can afford to have their own equipment in their homes.

Greek civilization, a period characterized by the highest form of literary creativity (Levarie, p. 9). The Greek empire experienced its greatest advancement under the leadership of Alexander the Great, a student of Aristotle. As the first classically educated world leader, Alexander placed a greater emphasis on the importance of libraries and education than had most of the earlier political and military leaders of the ancient world. In the Greek world Alexander wanted to recreate the glory of the Egyptian Pharaohs. He, therefore, placed the capital of his empire in Egypt. Although he did not live to see his new capital of Alexandria constructed, it was his idea which was to lead to the greatest library of the ancient Western world. The great library of Alexandria was founded by a Greek Pharaoh/King called Ptolemy I. It has been estimated that the library grew to over 700,000 scrolls (Gates, p. 11).

The first important libraries of the Roman empire were private collections and were usually of Greek origin. Those collections were often spoils of foreign conquests (Harris, p. 55). It was Julius Caesar who had the idea of public libraries for the Roman empire, but he died before it could be implemented (Gates, p. 13). The first public library in Rome was the Atrium Libertatis, founded in 37 B.C. by Asinius Pollio, a Roman politician (Harris, p. 57). The public libraries of the Roman period, however, should not be confused with the current public libraries. Very few people could read during the time of Julius Caesar. His concept of a public library was for the elite upper class of Rome, not for the common person.

The Medieval West

Invasions from the North led to the ultimate decline and collapse of the Roman empire and brought western civilization to a dark period. The western empire fell in the year 476 A.D., although the eastern empire would continue for another thousand years. During the time of turmoil of the Medieval era, little progress was made in the area of writing and preservation of written materials. It is possible that all classical literature might have disappeared without the dedicated work of a few foreign scholars such as Boethius and Cassiodorius.

The medieval scriptorium, or "library writing room," became the center for the preservation of written materials for Western Europe. During the early middle ages only those who were unable to work producing food for the survival of the monastery were sent to work in the scriptorium. The first scriptoria were outside buildings where there was no heat or artificial lighting to aid the monks in their daily tasks. The dirt floors were usually covered with straw and the monks sat on crude benches and worked on slanted desks. By the late middle ages the books being produced in the scriptoria had become a cash industry for the monastery (Olmert, p. 84). As a result the scriptorium became part of the main building complex and offered more comfort to the monks who produced books. For nearly one thousand years the typical library of Western Europe was a small collection of hand copied manuscripts. Those collections were cherished and guarded closely. The libraries contained religious material and were generally associated with a monastery or a cathedral school which educated priests.

The modern university began to develop in Europe during the eleventh century (Harris, p. 108). The first university to receive a charter was in Bologna, Italy. That university was established for the study of civil law and developed one of the early law libraries of Western Europe. The rise of libraries in universities occurred as a result of the collections of the university professors who eventually came to trust each other sufficiently to pool their own collections to form libraries for the university. Materials within the university libraries were guarded. Some libraries had a three lock method, which required three different professors to open the library. Books were often on chains sufficiently long enough to reach a nearby desk (Banks, p. 58). Only faculty and students were allowed in the library. Students could not enter the library unless they were wearing a cap and gown. Library rules forbade writing in books or tearing out the leaves. Talking in the library was strongly discouraged. An outsider who wanted to borrow a book had to make a deposit of equal value to replace the book in

INFORMATION AS POWER

Since the beginning of time, the person with information had power. Before the advent of the written word, those who kept the traditions of the tribe or clan had influence over others in that group. Many of the keepers of the word were the religious and political leaders. With the advent of the written word, those who were scribes had power because they could read and write. With the arrival of the moveable type printing press, more people had access to printed materials. But those who could read and write had special power over those who could not.

It is very evident in the world of cyberspace that those who have access to the information super-highway have power that others do not. Such advantage often translates into money, influence and power. In the modern world what really counts is the ability to acquire and use information.

case it was not returned. The university library collections were generally divided into three catego-ries -- theology, medicine, and law. Depending on the size and nature of the collections, other divi-sions might be devised.

As time went on a new group of businessmen began to collect around the new universities. Known as stationarii, they sold manuscripts to students (Harris, p. 109). These medieval book sellers employed a number of scribes to make copies for students. By the late middle ages some of the monastery scriptoria were producing books which were sold to the stationarii. These booksellers would either sell or rent books to students. Sometimes rental was by the page. A university text during the middle ages could cost the scholar the equivalent of hundreds of dollars.

The crowning glory of the medieval book world was the illuminated book, which began to appear by the sixth century. "Illuminations," decorative, often colorful, illustrations were added to texts to reveal or explain the content of the book. Illuminated books were very labor intensive and, as a result, were expensive. Only the wealthy could afford such books. Most of the illuminated books were religious in nature and used for prayers and meditation during the religious hours of the day. A large number were named either for the person who commissioned them or where they were pro-duced. For example, the *Book of Kells* was named for the monastery on the island of Iona, off the coast of Scotland, where it was produced (Avrin, p. 243).

LEGAL PROTECTION FOR CREATED WORKS

Almost all the materials in the library have a Ⓒ symbol on them while others have a Ⓡ symbol. Why is it there and what does it mean? The Ⓒ sym-bol is an indication of copyright protection and the Ⓡ symbol indicates a registered trademark. Those who create works, regardless of the medium, copy-right them to protect their own creative endeavors. The U.S. copyright law provides the creator, author, or publisher) of a work with protection for the life of the author plus fifty years.

Any time individuals use material from a copyrighted work within their own work, it is ethically important to give credit to the creator of the original work. Students may use information from a copyrighted work but must cite where they obtained the information. Likewise it is illegal to publish your own work using copyrighted information without first obtaining permission from the original creator.

The only protection given to a registered trademark is that it can not be used by others without permission. A good example of a registered trademark in a library is a Webster's dictionary. The only item protected in a Webster dictio-nary is the registered trademark: *Merriam-Webster* Ⓡ. Therefore, legally a person may borrow from the dictionary without giving credit to the creators, although he or she may not then create a new dictionary and use the registered trademark.

Early Modern Europe

The awakening of the Renaissance Period in Western Europe placed a great demand on the book world. The scriptoria of the monasteries and the book sellers and traders simply were unable to feed the ravenous appetite of the Renaissance scholars. As a result of this demand, businessmen began to seek out new methods to mass produce books. About half way through the fifteenth century a number of elements came together in the tinkering shop of Johannes Gutenberg of Mainz, Germany. Gutenberg was the creator of none of the elements, but he was able to bring them together to start the greatest revolution in human history: the moveable type printing press (Levarie, p. 77). The Chinese had developed paper making around the first century A.D. (Avrin, p. 283) and had been using, on a limited basis, moveable type printing methods since the eleventh century A.D. (Olmert, p. 65). Those two elements, along with a more pliable ink, came to the shop of Gutenberg and the movable printing press was created (Gates, p. 42). The first book to be printed on moveable type in Western Europe was the Gutenberg edition of the *Holy Bible* (Gates, p. 43). The new printing press was to play an important role in a religious, social, and political revolution during the sixteenth century known as the Reformation (Gates, p. 43).

By the seventeenth century a new library movement, the establishment of national libraries, had begun. All the countries of Western Europe began the development of what would become their national libraries. In France, the Royal Library was supplemented with the additions of private collections from wealthy people like Catherine de Medici. After the French Revolution the name of the library was changed to the Bibliotheque Nationale. The British Museum started the national library movement in England and the national library of Germany was known as the Imperial Library.

The Library Movement in the United States

There is no record to indicate the Pilgrims brought any books with them when they landed at Plymouth Rock. By 1629 Puritans had established a small collection of books for The Massachusetts Bay Colony. Throughout the English colonies in the new world a number of private library collections began to materialize. Among those individuals with substantial private library collections were, Benjamin Franklin of Philadelphia; Thomas Jefferson of Charlottesville, Virginia; The Byrd family of what would become West Virginia; Governor John Winthrop, Jr., of Connecticut; and Cotton Mather of Boston (Harris, p. 164-72). One of the first town libraries was established in Boston. A sea captain, Robert Keayne, left money in his will for a meeting house for the city of Boston which was to include a library (Marshall, p. 145).

There were a number of commercial attempts to provide library materials for the public. In 1731 Benjamin Franklin founded the Philadelphia Library Company (Wiegand & Davis, p. 356-7). In this voluntary association the members bought stock in the company and then paid an annual assessment to provide income for the purchase of books to be used by all members. That concept was known as a subscription library. A number of social libraries were developed in the colonies. These were generally organized along a knowledge base needed for a given profession. There were social libraries for those training to become members of a profession and for those who practiced in a profes-

> ## THINK ABOUT THIS...
>
> Were times that much different for a college student in the 1800's than they are right now? Many of the rules students followed then still exist. For example, a student in the 1800's could be expelled for carrying weapons and for damaging university property. Fines and expulsions were levied against students who were caught drunk, throwing water from a campus window or visiting houses of prostitution. Some differences, however, are evident. Be thankful that today you are not fined for talking too loud, singing, playing cards, swearing, missing lectures or winking in class.
>
> Collins, D. E., Catlett, D. B. & Collins, B. L. (1987). *Libraries and research: A practical approach*. Dubuque, IA: Kendall/Hunt. p. 18.

sion. Contemporary with the social libraries were circulating libraries. Unlike a subscription library, the circulating library was truly a commercial venture where the owner purchased books and then allowed others to use them for a fee (Harris, p. 184-9).

The national library for the United States came into existence after the War of 1812. The British Army had occupied Washington, D.C., and set fire to the capital building. That fire consumed the small library used by the members of the House of Representatives when seeking information to assist them with their duties of enacting legislation. Former president Thomas Jefferson was asked by the U.S. Congress to sell his library collection to replace the library lost in the capital building fire (Harris, p. 196). Jefferson, unlike current U.S. presidents, was not receiving any retirement benefits from the federal government and, because he was in need of cash to operate his estate, he agreed to sell his book collection. The collection of Jefferson became the foundation for what is today the world's largest library -- The Library of Congress. Parts of the Jefferson collection have been lost in three fires which struck the library, but much of the original collection still exists today.

The library of the eighteenth century was for the elite, the scholar, the man of learning, or the person who needed books for his occupation. There were no free public libraries for common citizens. Support for public libraries was a by-product of the universal public education movement. During the 1840's, public libraries gained important support through the efforts of Horace Mann (Harris, p. 189-90). He called for the housing of libraries in the public school buildings to be used by the public as well as the students. The first tax-supported city library was established in Peterborough, New Hampshire, in 1833 (Weigand & Davis, p. 519). The public library movement in Great Britain occurred at about the same time.

The major force behind the construction of public libraries in the United States was the Scotsman, Andrew Carnegie. At the age of eleven Carnegie came with his family to the United States. Carnegie's importance to the public library movement in the United States and Great Britain came as a result of the Carnegie Foundation which provided funds for 2,519 library buildings and collections. To qualify for the funding, a railroad town had to agree to vote a tax to support the maintenance of the building and the collection. If the town would do so, then the foundation gave them the money to construct the public library and to acquire a collection (Bobinski, p. vii, 195).

THE STUDENT'S RIGHT TO PRIVACY

While using the electronic catalog you discover "The Perfect Book" for your project. But it is checked out. It is not due back for ten days and your project is due in seven. You ask the student worker at the Circulation Desk to give you the name and address of the person who has the book checked out. "After all," you reason, "it has to be someone in my class and we can share the book." The student at the Circulation desk indicates that the libary is unable to provide that information. You argue that it is in the computer. He acknowledges that fact but still insist that the information can't be revealed because it would be a violation of the student's right to privacy.

Yes, students are afforded the right to privacy. It would be a violation of federal and state law for someone in the library to provide that information to you or any other person, including the police. This does not stop you, however, from asking aloud in class if someone has the book and if they are willing to share.

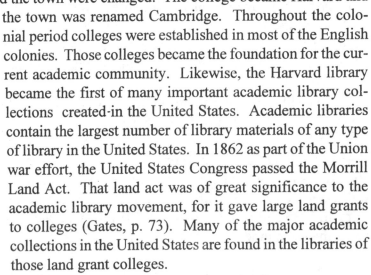

The academic library movement in the United States had its beginnings in 1636 when a new college was created in New Towne, Massachusetts. Like many others of the time, the college was created for the purpose of preparing young men to be ministers. Two years later, the will of John Harvard provided about 400 books to create a library for the college. Later, the names of both the college and the town were changed. The college became Harvard and the town was renamed Cambridge. Throughout the colonial period colleges were established in most of the English colonies. Those colleges became the foundation for the current academic community. Likewise, the Harvard library became the first of many important academic library collections created in the United States. Academic libraries contain the largest number of library materials of any type of library in the United States. In 1862 as part of the Union war effort, the United States Congress passed the Morrill Land Act. That land act was of great significance to the academic library movement, for it gave large land grants to colleges (Gates, p. 73). Many of the major academic collections in the United States are found in the libraries of those land grant colleges.

The twentieth century brought about great changes for colleges and universities. A large number of colleges and universities were created and more students attended and received degrees from institutions of higher learning.

THINK ABOUT THIS...

You are a very intelligent, industrious female who happens to live in the early 1800's. You are smarter than most of your male counterparts, yet you would not be allowed to attend any form of school, especially an institution of higher learning like Harvard. Why? Because the only jobs open to you would be those requiring little or no formal education. As a matter of fact you would be hard pressed to find a spouse, because no man would want someone smarter and better educated than himself. It makes the current times almost tolerable, doesn't it?

Collins, D. E., Catlett, D. B. & Collins, B. L. (1987). *Libraries and research: A practical approach*. Dubuque, IA: Kendall/Hunt Publishing Company, p. 18.

Academic library collections have experienced a phenomenal growth during the twentieth century. In addition those library collections have changed to include a number of non-print materials. Audio and video recordings became important elements of the academic collection. New formats, such as electronic resources, were added to academic collections. The print card catalog has been replaced by an electronic database. Likewise many of the print indexes for periodicals and newspapers have been replaced with information stored in electronic format, usually CD-ROM. Library collections have been supplemented by information sources available through computer networks such as the Internet. Individual academic library collections tend to support the programs offered by that university an provide a well-rounded collection of general information. With the current revolution in information technology academic libraries are in for a great amount of change. Within a few years much of an academic library collection may be available through computer networks as digital information. This would include full-text as well as indexing. The "paperless" society may be coming sooner than expected.

References

Avrin, L. (1991). *Scribes, script and books*. Chicago: American Library Association.

Banks, D. H. (1989). *Medieval manuscript bookmaking*. Metuchen, NJ: Scarecrow Press.

Bobinski, G. S. (1969). *Carnegie Libraries*. Chicago: American Library Association.

Bologna, G. (1988). *Illuminated manuscripts*. New York: Weidenfeld & Nicolson.

Canfora, L. (1987). *The vanished library*. Berkeley, CA: University of California Press.

Febvre, L. & Martin, H. (1990). *The coming of the book*. London: Verso.

Gates, J. K. (1990). *Introduction to librarianship*. New York: Neal-Schuman.

Harris, M. H. (1995). *History of libraries in the western world*. Metuchen, NJ: Scarecrow Press.

Levarie, N. (1968). *The art and history of books*. New York: James H. Heineman, Inc.

Marshall, D. N. (1983). *History of libraries ancient and mediaeval*. New Delhi: Oxford & IBH.

Olmert, M. (1992). *The Smithsonian book of books*. Washington D.C.: Smithsonian Books.

Vervliet, H. D. L. (1972). *The book through five thousand years*. New York: Phaidon.

Wiegand, W. (1996). Dewey declassified. *American Libraries, 27*(1), 54-56, 58, 60.

Wiegand, W. & Davis, D. G. (1994). *Encyclopedia of library history*. New York: Garland.

THE UNDERGRADUATE RESEARCH PAPER

Many college students consider writing research papers to be the biggest challenge facing them in school. The seemingly monumental task of writing 10, 15, or more pages on a topic can be made more manageable by breaking the project down into smaller pieces. It may be hard to believe now, but research papers get easier to write once the student gains experience.

The Library Research Process

Organization is a primary key to success when writing a research paper. Those who develop a plan and then follow that plan will be more effective and efficient. If the library research process is approached without a plan it is often evident in the final product. One important element of an effective plan is the development of a calendar of events. Such a schedule assists the researcher in meeting deadlines by organizing the steps needed to complete the assignment. The time necessary to develop a calendar of events will pay big dividends throughout the research project. Not everyone will be able to stay on schedule, but those with a schedule generally complete their assignment in a more efficient manner and often receive a higher grade on the research paper.

The following suggested steps for writing the undergraduate research paper provides a framework for developing a research strategy:

1. Select a topic
2. Develop a thesis or problem statement
3. Create an outline
4. Develop a search strategy
5. Prepare to write or present

Select a Topic

A common downfall for many students is a failure to think through the process of selecting a topic. Spending time at the beginning of the process in selecting an appropriate topic will save time and avoid later complications. Therefore, the decision about which topic to research should not be taken lightly. The selection of a topic should be based on careful investigation of the subject.

Some instructors allow the student great flexibility in the selection of a topic, while others will be more restrictive. During the topic selection process the following items should be considered:

Is the topic of interest?
Will the topic meet the requirements of the assignment?
Is sufficient information available on the topic?
Can information be collected and organized on the topic within the time allotted?

Almost any topic could *conceivably* be researched; however, some topics are just plain bad ideas for undergraduate students who have just a few weeks. Some topics require months of research and a paper hundreds of pages long to do it justice. Other topics may have little published information about it in the library. If a student must choose his or her own topic, there are a number of ways to think of a good one. One can browse through newspapers, magazines or journals. Students can also brainstorm with each other, with their instructor or with reference librarians to get ideas.

Whether the instructor assigns topics, allows students to select from a list, or lets them choose one on his or her own, it is always a good idea to *conduct some background reading before proceeding with the research paper*. When selecting a topic, the student should look at some general reference works such as encyclopedias. Academic libraries have a variety of general and subject encyclopedias which provide the student with an introduction to the subject area. At least an introductory search should be made of the library's electronic catalog and of periodical, newspaper and other appropriate indexes. Students then will better understand what they're getting into and will know if the university library has sufficient information available to support the topic.

Another very common problem students have is choosing too broad a topic. When a broad topic is chosen, the researcher may discover that there are a huge number of resources that could be used. It is a difficult chore to wade through hundreds of possible references to find the best ones. A broad topic is also difficult to channel into a coherent research paper because the researcher tries to include too much information. A paper on a concise, well-defined topic that has sufficient published material available is much easier to research and write. Figure 2.1 shows how to narrow a topic.

Develop a Thesis or Research Problem

An effective undergraduate research paper should have direction and purpose. The primary element in providing focus for a paper will be a thesis or research problem. The word "thesis" some-

Figure 2.1

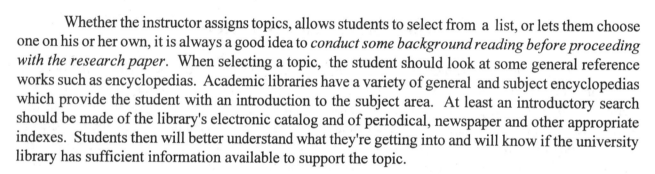

Broad Topic —————————————— **Narrow Topic**

Athletics

Bicycling
  - Tour de France
  - Greg Lemond
  - Bicycling and women's mobility in the 19th century

Baseball
  - Training infielders
  - Treating shoulder injuries
  - Baseball as a social equalizer

times refers to the research paper written by graduate students, but a more generic definition refers to the core subject of any paper. The thesis poses a statement of fact or position on the topic. A problem statement is similar, except it is usually posed as a question. For example, if a student decided to write about the effect of slavery on the antebellum (pre-Civil War) economy, a thesis statement could be, "Reliance on slavery as an institution *caused* the collapse of the antebellum economy." The thesis makes a statement of fact, which will be supported and proven throughout the paper. An example of a problem statement would be, "*To what extent* did the reliance on slavery cause an economic decline during the antebellum period?" The problem statement poses a question about the same topic. From a thesis or problem statement flows the other elements of organization for the research paper. Writing a paper lacking such a focus will often result in a paper without direction and purpose and frequently results in a lower grade.

Create an Outline

Although it is the thesis statement which provides direction, it is the outline which supports that thesis and brings organization to the research paper. A paper may be written from a variety of approaches. For example, a paper about the presidency of James Earl Carter might be outlined *chronologically*, providing a presentation of the events of the Carter presidency in the order of occurrence. This approach might be easy to organize but might not be the best method to deal with the subject. An outline which explores the *major topics* of the Carter administration might be a more logical approach, incorporating such items as the economy, international relations, and domestic politics. Another approach to outlining a paper dealing with the Carter administration might be *thematic*: Jimmy Carter as world peace maker, as the moral leader of America, as a micro manager of government, etc.

A thematic outline could be arranged as follows:

Thesis: James Earl Carter was an effective/ineffective president. (Choose your position ahead of time through initial readings.)

 A. Carter as world peace maker
   1. negotiation of the hostage crisis
   2. development of the Sadat/ Begin relationship

 B. Carter as moral leader of America

 C. Carter as a manager of government
   1. relationship with Congress
   2. changes in the Supreme Court
   3. changes in the federal government bureaucracy

It is important to develop an outline for a research paper *before* beginning the search for materials to support the thesis and outline. You cannot make up the paper 's outline as you write the paper. If the research paper shows no direction or purpose, it will be of poor quality. Without a thesis and an outline student efforts will not result in a high quality paper.

Develop a Search Strategy

After a thesis is determined and the outline developed, the researcher will decide on a logical strategy to locate supporting information. The search for information will begin with what was discovered during the preliminary search of the library catalog and indexes. Book materials will not always provide the best information for college level research. A search of periodical indexes (magazines and journals) may be more profitable in providing supporting evidence. It is critical to perform some sort of evaluation of the sources you are using. Examining the author(s) and their motives for producing the material can be very enlightening.

When an appropriate source is located it is important to take detailed notes. Effective research is dependent upon good note-taking. Notes should indicate clearly whether the information is a summary of what was read or a direct quote. Such indications on note cards assist the researcher to avoid plagiarism. Since the information contained on those note cards is not the student's original thoughts, it is important that appropriate credit be given to the sources. Notations should be made for quotes, statistics or any information not considered to be common knowledge. In addition, the researcher needs to collect all necessary information to prepare the bibliography or list of references. When using library materials, be sure that the information needed for the bibliography is recorded before the item is returned to the library shelves. In other words, make sure you have a complete title, author(s), volume numbers, and page number(s) written down for everything you used. One way to insure that the necessary information is obtained is to make a photocopy of the title page or other pages containing such information.

Preparing to Write or Present

Once a sufficient amount of information has been collected to support the elements of the outline for the research paper, it is time to organize for the writing process. The more time spent preparing information to fit within the outline, the more efficient will be the writing process.

Information from library materials can be incorporated into the paper in different ways. It can be directly quoted, paraphrased, or summarized. Quotes are placed in the paper word-for-word as they appeared in the original work. Quotes must be set off in quotation marks, or set off in a block of text. Paraphrasing and summarizations are looser interpretations of the original material.

When the first draft has been completed the most valuable gift available for the researcher is the gift of time, time to do other things before coming back to the research paper. Time will allow the researcher to return to the paper with a fresh approach. If this isn't possible, then the next best thing is to have other people read the paper. It is important to select persons who are knowledgeable about the English language and the writing process. The researcher should plan to write at least two drafts of the paper before considering the paper complete.

When the final draft has been completed, the research paper is still not ready to be submitted. It is important to remember packaging. Have the paper printed on good quality paper with a laser rather than a dot matrix printer. Include a cover page that states the name of the assignment, instructor, your name, and date. A very large project may look nice in a folder or binder. Always follow the instructor's directions, however, as some instructors find folders annoying.

Remember: Some instructors may not accept late papers; therefore, it is always a good idea to allow time in your calendar of events to get the paper in early, or at least on time!

Time Management

To summarize, let's go back to the idea of developing a calendar of events. To reduce the anxiety that a major assignment creates, don't procrastinate. Begin planning as soon as the assignment is given by setting several deadlines that correspond to the paper-writing process.

Select a Topic: Plan to spend a couple hours or an afternoon in the library exploring possibilities and testing various topics against the kinds of books and other materials available. Include time to brainstorm with friends and a librarian. Once you have a general idea of what kinds of materials are available, think about the thesis or research problem to focus later research efforts. This part of the process may happen as you explore your topic, or it may require a second trip to the library.

Prepare an Outline: The outline will guide your writing as you lead your reader from the introduction to the conclusion. This, too, may develop as you explore library resources or reflect later on the materials you found. The outline may grow and change as you research your topic.

Research the Topic: Guided by your outline, begin reading about the subject. Set aside time to discuss your topic with a librarian who can suggest a variety of resources that support your research. Again, don't put off this part of the process. If you need to request materials from another library, the interlibrary loan process will take several days. Do this work early to allow yourself time to wait for materials or to develop an alternate plan.

Write: Plan to complete your first draft several days before the due date. Let it rest for a day or two, then, with fresh eyes, rewrite again and again until you are content enough to call it finished.

If you follow this plan, you will find that you have time to reflect on your topic, to adjust your schedule for the unexpected, and possibly to enjoy the process.

Documenting Library Research

This section offers a selection of general and special style manuals available and shows how they are used to document works in your research paper. This book focuses on "APA" bibliographic style developed by the American Psychological Association.

What is a style manual? A style manual explains how to construct research papers using a uniform format and to credit research sources using footnotes or endnotes and a bibliography or references page. There are many different ways of citing sources. It is important to be consistent throughout a paper in your style of presenting and citing the information. Choose a style and stick to it throughout the paper. Since each instructor or department may adopt a different style manual, you should ask about a preferred style before beginning the paper.

Footnotes, endnotes, or in-text notation are used to identify the source of a particular quotation or the original ideas borrowed from a published or unpublished source. Basically, anything that is not your original idea must be acknowledged. Footnotes are placed at the bottom of the page and endnotes are placed at the end of the paper or chapter of the work. In-text notation places the author's name and date right into the text, referring the reader to a list of references at the end of the paper. Bibliographies or references are a list of all sources that were used in compiling the paper -- not just those used for direct quotes, but for all materials paraphrased or summarized, too, including books, articles, newspapers, videos, etc.

The basic differences between the various bibliographic styles are the indentation, the order in which the authors' names are written, and capitalization of various elements. Footnotes and endnotes refer to specific sections or pages, while entries on a bibliography or references page cite the entire work. Style manuals can be found in a library's online catalog by searching under the subject headings: Authorship, Report Writing, or Technical Writing. Also, you can search the online catalog using specific subjects followed with the word "authorship" as a subheading. For example:

Children's literature--Authorship
Nursing -- Authorship
Social Sciences -- Authorship

The following is a list of more commonly used style manuals. Like dictionaries, they are essential aids to writing term papers and would be wise investments regardless of your field of specialization.

The Chicago manual of style (14th ed.). (1993). Chicago: University of Chicago Press.

Gibaldi, J. (1995). *MLA handbook for writers of research papers* (4th ed.). New York: Modern Language Association of America.

Hacker, D. (1994). *The Bedford handbook for writers* (4th ed.). Boston: Bedford Books.

Publication manual of the American Psychological Association (4th ed.). (1994). Washington, DC: American Psychological Association.

Slade, C., Campbell, W., and Ballou, S. (1994). *Form and style: Research papers, reports, theses* (9th ed.). Boston: Houghton Mifflin.

Turabian, K. (1987). *A manual for writers of term papers, theses and dissertations* (5th ed.). Chicago: University of Chicago Press.

MLA and APA Footnote and Bibliographic Entries

The following examples show the differences between sample footnote and bibliography entries for MLA and APA style manuals.

Notes - APA
Instead of using footnotes, APA uses the author-date method of citation within the text of the docu-

CASE IN POINT

Professor Marnholtz assigned a five page paper, with citations and references, on any aspect of diversity in American society. The class was divided into groups for the project. Zachary, Elise and Dudley became a group. They agreed that it might be best if each one of the group checked the library for articles on diversity. Elise found an interesting article by J. William Harris, "Etiquette, Lynching, and Racial Boundaries in Southern History: A Mississippi Example," in the June 1995 issue of the *American Historical Review*.

Unfortunately, when the group finally got together, neither Zach or Dudley had found anything. After a few minutes of discussion it was clear they did not have a plan. Elise indicated that the article in the *American Historical Review* would be a good place to start.

Zach said, "I'll tell you what we can do. Professor Marnholtz wants a five page article on diversity. We'll give him one. All we have to do is just copy from this article." Dudley inquired "Can we do that?" "Why not!" demanded Zach. Dudley asked, "Isn't that plagiarism?" He continued, "How about writing an article *based* on this article and cite the sources from the footnotes." "Wait a minute," interrupted Elise, "that's not right either. We can only use *those* sources if we have read them!" "Now hold on, Elise. We don't have time to do that. Let's just write our paper and use the sources from the article," replied Dudley. Zach thought for a moment and then stated, "Let's just copy from this article and turn it in. You know that Marnholtz will never check to see whether we wrote the article or if we used original sources."

What should the group do? Does the university have a policy about this?

Are there legal or moral implications to what Zach and Dudley are suggesting?

What can Elise do, since she does not agree with this plan?

ment. Therefore, the surname of the author and the year of publication are stuck right into the text at the appropriate point. For example:

```
Tygett, Small, and Slattery (1996) found several types ....
.... as Medaris and Lanuzo (1995a) demonstrated in their ....
Three studies (M. Lawson, 1995; L. Peery, 1994; Antrim, 1992) are ...
```

At the end of the paper there must be an entry in the list of references to provide the full citation information.

Footnotes - MLA

The MLA style encourages the use of endnotes instead of footnotes, unless your instructor specifies footnotes. MLA endnotes have the first line indented. Examples of a variety of MLA endnotes are shown in the next section.

¹John W. Little, <u>Student's Guide for Writing College Papers</u> 3rd ed. (Chicago: University of Chicago Press, 1976) 48.

²Leslie Lynam, "Winning With Your Sword," <u>Psychology Today</u> Nov.-Dec. 1995: 84.

Bibliographies

Bibliographies provide almost the same information as footnotes and endnotes. The only difference is the the addition of page numbers. Some of the more noticeable differences between MLA and APA are capitalization, underlining, punctuation marks, use of initials, and the way author's names are reported. Below are simple examples of APA and MLA style that illustrate their differences. A more complete listing of APA-style citations appears on pages 19-24. For full information, consult the appropriate style manual.

Book - MLA

Jones, Wilbur and Jan Smit. <u>Why Can't We All Just Get Along</u>. New York: International Universities Press, 1986.

Book- APA

Jones, W. and Smit, J. (1986). <u>Why can't we all just get along.</u> New York: International Universities Press.

Journal Article - MLA

Humphries, John W. "Where's the Beef?" <u>American Journal of Clinical Nutrition</u> 23 (1985): 522-533.

Journal Article - APA

Humphries, J. W. (1985). Where's the beef? <u>American Journal of Clinical Nutrition, 23</u> 522-533.

Internet Resources

Land, T. (1996, November 25). *Web Extension to American Psychological Association Style* (WEAPAS) (Rev. 1.2.4) [Online]. Available http://www.beadsland.com/weapas

Walker, J. R. (1995, April). *Walker/ACW style sheet; MLA-style citations of electronic sources* [Online]. Available http://www.cas.usf.edu/english/walker/mla.html

APA References

The next several pages provide examples in APA format for citing many different kinds of materials. Students will find these examples particularly helpful in completing assignments.

The sample references below are representative of typical entries. If you use a source for which there is no specific example, please consult the APA manual [*Publication Manual of the American Psychological Association* (4th ed.). (1994). Washington, DC: The Association.]. If you still do not find an example, review the general forms and follow the one that most resembles your source. Remember, when in doubt, it is always best to include more information than needed than not enough. One of the main reasons for listing references is to provide the reader with enough information to also retrieve the sources. References in APA format are typed single spaced using a hanging indent and alphabetized by the first element in each entry. Note: search statements [in brackets] are for this class only. Do not include them in your reference lists for other classes.

Books (and other nonperiodicals)

General Form

```
Author, A.A. (1994). Title of work: Be sure to include subtitle. City, ST:
    Publisher.
```

Elements

Author: Authors' names inverted; surname, and intials only.

Title: Title in **Limited capitals**, first word and proper nouns capitalized. Also capitalize the first word after a colon.

Location: Use city and state, **use two letter postal abbreviations for state.** (Use city only for New York, Baltimore, Boston, Chicago, Los Angeles, Philadelphia, San Francisco, and London. Complete listing in APA manual) Cite only the first city listed on title page.

Publisher: Write out names of associations, corporations, and universities. Omit terms such as "Publishers", "Co.", or "Inc." Retain "Books" and "Press."

Examples

```
Ainsle, R. C. (1995). The psychology of twinship. Lincoln, NE: University
    of Nebraska Press.
    [Found in the online catalog under "Twins"]

Ambs, A. (1969). Makin' bacon: The beginner's guide to animal husbandry.
    Springfield, MI: McCully Books.
    [Found in the online catalog under "swine"]

Smith, J. D. (1988). Psychological profiles of conjoined twins: Heredity
    environment, and identity. New York: Praeger.
    [Found in the online catalog under "Twins"]
```

Article In Edited Book

General Form

Author, A. A., & Author, B.B. (1995). Title of chapter. In A. Editor, B.
Editor, & C. Editor (Eds.), <u>Title of book</u> (pp. xxx-xxx). City, ST:
Publisher.

Elements

Multiple authors: Separate with commas; insert ampersand (&) before final author.

Title: Use no quotation marks around titles of articles. Underline title of book or periodical. Add
edition statement (2nd ed.) after title.

Editors: Do not invert editor's names. Finish editor statement with a comma.

Page Numbers: Give inclusive page numbers of article or chapter in parentheses after title.

Examples

Signed article in an edited book

Hartley, J. T., Harker, J. O., & Walsh, D. A. (1990). Contemporary issues
and new directions in the development of twins. In L. W. Jones (Ed.),
<u>Psychological issues in the rearing of twins</u> (pp. 239-252). Washington,
DC: American Psychological Association.
[Found in <u>Bibliographic Index</u> (1986) under "Twins"]

Entry in an encyclopedia authored by one person

Berghoff, M. B. (1977). Cold fusion. In <u>The chemistry encyclopedia</u> (Vol.
14, pp. 327-330). Chicago: Waldrums.
[Found in the online catalog using "Chemistry and encyclopedia"]

Edited book

Gibson, J. V., & Jones, L. (Eds.). (1992). <u>Can you believe what you see: A
story of disbelief.</u> Kansas City, MO: Hughes.
[Found in LUIS under "Gibson.au."]

Slade, E. (Ed.). (1992). <u>The dictionary of music and sound</u> (6th ed., Vols.
1-16). London: Macmillan.
[Found in the online catalog under "music and dictionary"]

Book, revised edition, Jr. in name

Juel-Neilson, N., Jr. (1990). <u>Individual and environment: Monozygotic
twins reared apart</u> (Rev. ed.). New York: Universities Press.
[Found in the online catalog under "Twins"]

Book, no author or editor

<u>Merriam-Webster's dictionary</u> (9th ed.). (1988). New York: Merriam-Webster.
[Found in the online catalog under "dictionary"]

Book, group author (government agency) as publisher also

Australian Bureau of Statistics. (1991). <u>Child psychology in the Outback, June 1994</u> (No. 3857). Canberra, Australian Capital Territory: Author.
[Found in the online catalog under "child psychology and Australia"]

Periodicals

General Form

Author, A. A., Author, B. B., & Author, C. C. (1994). Title of article. <u>Title of Periodical, vol,</u> pages.

Elements

> **Date:** For **professional journals** enter only the year of the volume. For **magazines and newspapers**, give year followed by month and day, if any.

> **Author:** If no author is indicated, begin entry with the title of the article, followed by the date.

> **Volume Numbers:** For **professional journals** and **magazines,** type the volume number and underline it. Do not use "Vol." before the number. For **professional journals,** if and only if each issue begins on page 1, give the issue number in parentheses immediately after the volume number.

> **Page Numbers:** Give the inclusive page numbers. Use "p." or "pp." before the page number only in reference to **newspapers**, not professional journals, magazines, or newsletters. Use a comma between page numbers to denote nonconsecutive paging.

Examples

Journal

Bouchard, T. (1993). Do environmental similarities explain the similarity in intelligence of identical twins reared apart? <u>Intelligence, 7,</u> 325-356.
[Found in ProQuest under "Twins reared apart"]

Journal article, two authors (each issue begins on p. 1)

Klimoski, R., & Palmer, S. (1996). The ADA and the hiring process. <u>Consulting Journal,45</u> (2), 11-22.
[Found in <u>Business Periodicals Index</u> (March 1996) under "ADA"]

Journal article, three to five authors

Borr, W. A., Smith, J., Johnson, O., & White, P. E. (1996). Supervisor for now. <u>Psychology Vision, 78,</u> 339-345.
[Found in Psyclit using "supervisor"]

Magazine

Sean, D. (1994, January). I always knew I had a double. <u>Redbook, 24,</u> 26.
[Found in Readers' Guide to Periodical Literature (1994) under "twins"]

Newspaper

Bryant, J. (1990, September 19). Fellow students unite brothers. <u>The New York Times,</u> pp. A1, A4.
    [Found in <u>New York Times Index </u>(1990) under "Multiple Births"]

NewsBank (from microfiche)

Klapper, E. (1994, October 19). Twin's moms receive advice at convention. <u>Palm Beach</u> [FL] <u>Post, NewsBank,</u> Welfare and Social Problems, 1994, 76:B4.
    [Found in NewsBank Index (CD-ROM) under "Twins"]

NewsBank (from full text CD-ROM)

Lenhard, E. (1996, February 13). Who's reading your e-mail? Interception of messages causes computer users to wonder about secuting [CD-ROM]. <u>Atlanta</u> [GA] <u>Constitution</u>, p. D1. NewsBank NewsFile Record No. 00803*19960213*00105.
    [Found in NewsBank (full text CD-ROM) under "Internet and freedom of information"]

Miscellaneous Examples

Encyclopedia (edited book, article signed by author)

Breslin, F. C. (1992). Individual differences. In R. J. Corsisni (Ed.), <u>Encyclopedia of psychology</u> (Vol. 2, pp. 196-197). New York: John Wiley & Sons.
    [Found in the online catalog under "Psychology-Dictionaries"]

Biographical (edited book, article unsigned by author)

Kallman, Franz Joseph. (1992). In R. M. Godenson (Ed.), <u>Longman dictionary of psychology and psychiatry</u> (p. 402). New York: Longman.
    [Found in the online catalog under "Psychology--Dictionaries"]

Government Document, Corporate author

National Institute of Mental Health. (1992). <u>Cancer in mothers of dizygotic twins</u>. Washington, DC: U.S. Government Printing Office.
    [Found in GPO Monthly Catalog [CD-ROM] under "Twins"]

Government Document, with report number

McNeeley, T. (1990). <u>Development of behavioral techniques to control hyperaggressiveness in young children</u> (CYC Report No. 80-3562). Washington, DC: Council on Young Children. (NTIS No. PB80-143282)
    [Found in NTIS [CD-ROM] under "Twins"]

ERIC document

Franke, R. H. (1993). <u>Environmental sources of intelligence differences among separated identical twins.</u> Paper presented at the Annual Convention of the American Psychological Association, Toronto, Canada. (ERIC Document Reproduction Service No. ED 251 245)
[Found in ERIC under "Twins reared apart"]

Book Review

Jones, R. C. (1987). Living with twins [Review of the book <u>Two or more</u>]. <u>American Journal of Pediatrics, 32,</u> 233, 267.
[Found in <u>Cumulative Index to Nursing & Allied Health Literature</u> (1988) under "Multiple Births--Book Reviews"]

Videotape

Lovett, L. (Producer), & Roberts, J. (Director). (1995). <u>I wish Julia had a twin</u> [videotape]. Hollywood, CA: Warner Bros.
[Found in the online catalog using "Twins and f.fmt."]

Unpublished paper presented at meeting

Key, T. (1989, April). <u>Rearing twins in an urban environment</u>. Paper presented at the meeting of the Missouri Health Association, Warrensburg, MO.
[Found in Vertical File under "Twins"]

Dissertation

Painter, C. R. (1982). An analysis of behaviors of twins in varios classroom situations (Doctoral dissertation, University of Missouri, 1981). <u>Dissertation Abstracts International, 42,</u> 5603A. (University Microfilms No. 84-07, 234)
[Found on <u>Dissertation Abstracts Ondisc</u> (July 1980-December 1984) under "Multiple Births"]

Music Recording

Grimwood, K., & Idlet, E. (1990). Two brains [Recorded by A. Couple]. On <u>Trout fishing in America: Truth is stranger than fishin'</u> [CD]. Houston, TX: Trout Records.
[Found in <u>Music Index</u> (1991) under "Twins"]

Online journal, general access (E-mail)

Funder, D. C. (1994, March). Judgmental process and content: Commentary on twins [9 paragraphs]. <u>Psycholquy</u> [Online serial], <u>5</u>(17). Available E mail: psyc@pucc Message: Get psyc 94-xxxxx.
[Found on Internet under psyc@pucc, Get psyc 94-xxxx"]

Internet - WWW or gopher

Abelman, J.A. (1996). Going to the trouble to get it [Online]. Available:
    http://amber.mizzou.mu.edu Path: Library services/A belman
    [Found in Yahoo using search term "trouble"]

Central Missouri State University, Office of Institutional Research.
    (1996). Academic discipline profiles: University 1000 [Online]. Avail-
    able: gopher://cmsuvmb.cmsu.edu:70/11/cmsu/testfact/testdisp/testprov/
    univ1000.testprov

Goldschmidt, A. & Akera, A. (1996). John W. Mauchly and the Development of
    the ENIAC Computer. An Exhibition in the Department of Special Collec-
    tions Van Pelt Library, University of Pennsylvania [Online]. Available:
    http://www.library.upenn.edu/special/gallery/mauchly/jwmintro.html
    [Found in Excite using search terms "Internet" and "history"

3

LIBRARY CATALOGS AND CLASSIFICATION SYSTEMS

In libraries, books and materials are usually grouped or classified according to their subject matter. Most college and university libraries will use one or more classification systems to organize materials. Some common library classification schemes are the following: Dewey Decimal System, Library of Congress Classification, and Superintendent of Documents Classification.

Some libraries use other systems of classification or even create their own. Many college and university libraries organize the majority of their materials using the Library of Congress Classification. Dewey Decimal classification is commonly used in public libraries and in school libraries. A library may use more than one system. For example, a collection of federal government publications may be classified using Superintendent of Documents Classification.

Any item that is classified in a library collection is assigned a call number that is usually labeled on the spine of a book or elsewhere for other formats of materials. The first portion of a call number for books or other materials is the subject classification number. The remainder of a call number will usually have an author number or book number which identifies a specific work within a subject classification. Multiple volumes or copies in a library may have identical call numbers, but all works with different titles should have a unique call number for that title.

The Library of Congress Classification System

Library of Congress Classification is a system of letters and numbers which was originally designed to organize the library of the Congress of the United States. It has been adopted by many academic libraries in

---

THINK ABOUT THIS....

The organization of like items into groups is a common practice which makes finding them easier. Many of us organize our dresser drawers so that we have a sock drawer and a sweater drawer. Our closets may be arranged so that blouses or shirts hang together, with skirts or trousers grouped likewise. Our shoes may be arranged so that the casual shoes are at the front of our storage space and our dress shoes are to the rear. Cans in a pantry may be placed so that all soups are together on a shelf, vegetables are next, and cans of fruit are on yet another shelf. They may also be arranged according to the size of the can. The CLASSIFICATION of objects according to some common factor is practiced daily in our lives.

the United States as a uniform system for classifying topics. Each item in a library collection is assigned a unique classification number. When placed in order, all items of similar subjects are together on the shelf.

The first portion of a call number for a work classified using this system will have one or two letters. For example, you may see a *D, QA, or RT* which broadly groups the materials into a subject area such as History, Data Processing, or Nursing. See Figure 3.1 for a list of the major Library of Congress subject divisions. The letter portion is followed by numbers which further subdivide the broad subject area,

Figure 3.1

Library of Congress Classification Classes

A	General Works
AE	Encyclopedias
AY	Almanacs
B-BJ	Philosophy, Psychology, Mythology, Ethics
BL-BX	Religion
C	Auxiliary Sciences of History, Archaeology
D	History: Africa, Asia, Europe, Oceania
E	History: American
F	History: Canada and Latin America
G	Geography,
GN	Anthropology
GR-GV	Recreation, Sports, Folklore, Customs
H	Social Sciences
HB-HG	Economics, Management, Marketing, Finance
HQ	Family, Women
HV	Criminology
J	Political Science
K	Law
KF	Law of the United States
L	Education
M	Music
N	Fine Arts
P	Languages and Linguistics
PR, PS	English and American Literature, Fiction in English
Q	Sciences: Mathematics, Physics, Chemistry, Geology, Biology
R	Medicine
S	Agriculture
T	Technology: Engineering, Construction
TL	Transportation, Aviation
TX	Home Economics
U	Military Science
V	Naval Science
Z	Bibliography, Library Science

perhaps by specific country, time period, or type. The third part of the call number is a letter and number combination which is called a book or author number. This part alphabetizes works on like subjects by their authors or, in some cases, by titles. The last part of a Library of Congress call number is the publication date of the work. The date allows different editions of the same title to be identified one from the other. See Figure 3.2 for examples of a Library of Congress call number.

When looking for a book classified by the Library of Congress system, all numbers before a decimal point (in the first alpha-numeric sequence) are read in whole number sequence. Every number after the first alpha-numeric sequence (except the date) is read as a decimal. Thus, LB3508.5 M35 will come before LB3509 C42. On the shelf, books are arranged according to their classification and within each class, alphabetically by the author's name.

Below is a sample of some Library of Congress call numbers. Put each row in correct order. At the bottom of the Figure is the correct number for the order of each entry. Try it and see how you do.

TRY THIS....

Row A	AE54 .N5531	AG105.4 .L55	A20 .A2	AE5 .N553	AN 1 .N76	AE541 .L55
Row B	CR 131 U3	CR21 .B7	CS248.1 .S55	C 76.5 A5	CS 2481 S55	C32 .B76
Row C	P462.5 .A3 1925	PE 1580 S5	PC2689 .V4 1969	P2689 .R27	PC2689 .V4	P 4625 A34
Row D	D56 .R15	DA360 .A6	DA40 B6	DD 360 A14	D56 .R2 1917	D56.2 .A8
Row E	HA25.4 .B67	HA 254 A46	HA254 .Z9 1954	HA254 .Z24	HF 505 Z2	HA254 .Z9 1961

Answers: Row A 3, 5, 1, 2, 6, 4   Row D 1, 5, 4, 6, 2, 3
Row B 4, 3, 5, 2, 6, 1   Row E 1, 2, 4, 3, 6, 5
Row C 1, 6, 5, 2, 4, 3

The Dewey Decimal System

The Dewey Decimal System is a numerical subject classification system which groups all information into ten major categories such as 300 for Social Sciences, 400 for languages, 500 for Science, and 800 for literature. The numeric portion can contain a decimal number in order to subdivide a subject into ever more specific portions. Consequently, a Dewey Decimal classification number can be quite long.

In a call number of a book classified in the Dewey system, the author or book number follows the Dewey classification number. It serves the same purpose as the author number in the Library of Congress system. The author or book number puts titles on the same subject in alphabetical order and may be used to to distinguish different editions of the same work.

Figure 3.2

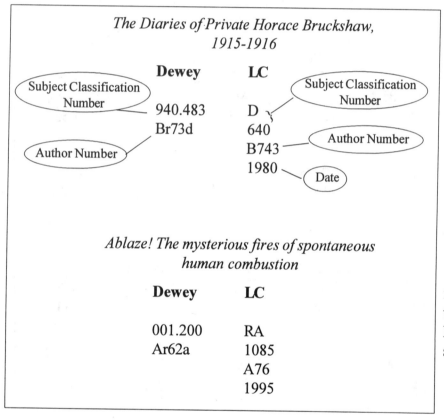

On the shelf, a Dewey call number is read decimally until a letter appears as part of the call number. Following the numeric portion, the remainder of the call number, the author number, is alphabetically sequenced for the letters and numerically sequenced for the numbers which follow the letters. There is no decimal arrangement of the author number.

Figure 3.2 illustrates the differences in a call number using the Library of Congress and Dewey Decimal Systems of classification.

The Superintendent of Documents Classification System

One other major classification scheme is used to organize materials in the libraries of many colleges and universities. That is the Superintendent of Documents classification. It is used to group the publications of the U.S. Government Printing Office. It is not an arrangement of subject categories but a system which designates the government agency which is responsible for the particular publication. Consequently, publications of the Department of Commerce will begin with a *C* and those from the Department of Agriculture begin with *A*. On occasion the beginning letter has no relationship at all to the government body from which it emanates. For example, the call number for publications for legislative materials from Congress begin with a *Y*. The letter portion of the classification is followed with numbers and more letters which further subdivide the agency. The punctuation is part of the classification scheme and may include colons, slashes, dashes, and periods.

Because documents are arranged by government agency rather than subject, a person can not go to a single place to browse all the documents on a particular subject. Government documents are best accessed by an indexing tool, such as the online catalog (which may not have complete coverage) or a government documents catalog.

Each publication from the Government Printing Office is assigned its own unique number. Even each issue of a periodical has a slightly different classification number from the other issues. Each issue shares the broad classification portion; it is the final part indicating the specific issue that is different. In such a way, each item has a unique call number so it can be shelved in a logical fashion and retrieved by the use of the classification number. The examples in Figure 3.3 are of Superintendent of Documents call numbers from actual government documents.

Figure 3.3

North Carolina's Forests, 1990	A13.80:SE-142
Sexual Harassment on the Job	CR1.6/2:H21
Washington Architecture, 1791-1861	FT1.8/2:F96/2

Each state has its own state government publications and may have its own classification system. For example, Missouri state publications have a classification number which is similar in appearance to the Superintendent of Documents call number.

The examples of call numbers for Missouri state documents in Figure 3.4 illustrate their state documents classification numbers.

Figure 3.4

State of Missouri Financial Summary	MO AD.Ac10:
Missouri Christmas Tree Buyer's Guide	MO AG4:C46
Taste Missouri Wine Country	MO AG 4:W63

Library Catalogs

Library users need to be able to identify the items in a library and figure out where they are housed. At first libraries created lists of the books that they owned. As libraries grew the lists were printed into books, and book catalogs were created. Because of the difficulty in updating these catalogs as new materials were added to a library, a card catalog evolved. Each item in a library was carefully described on a 3" X 5" card, providing users with the essential information needed to identify the work. Usually this consisted of the author(s) or group which was treated as an author, the title, place of publication and publisher's name, and the date of publication. Additional information gave the number of pages, mentioned any illustrations, and gave the height of the book in centimeters.

One may wonder why librarians would care about the height of a book at all, but the purpose was to assure that the work would fit on a standard sized book shelf. If you notice a shelf of books in any library, the majority of the books are within a very similar range in height. Very large or small books require special accommodation on book shelves and, therefore, may be shelved on special shelves.

Other information about a specific book or other materials was added to the card as needed. For example, a listing of the contents from the table of contents, perhaps some piece of information specific only to that particular copy or a note that the book was autographed by the author might be included. Additionally, the classification number for the book, including its unique author number, was added so that a call number applied to only that title in a library. The last pieces of information included on a catalog card were headings identifying the subject matter of the work, names of other authors who were major creators of the book, and the name of a series which grouped this particular title with other titles that shared something in common.

As the age of computers developed, libraries were one of the first organizations to see the value of placing all this information into a computerized data base. By doing this, a person can search for books or other materials on a topic, by an author, or by title. A very complex method of translating the standard information about each work into computer data was developed in the late 1960's and early 1970's. While not every library that exists today has moved from a card catalog to a computerized catalog or online catalog, the card catalog is very much fading from use.

Unfortunately, one of the results of this change from a card catalog to a computer catalog is a loss of standardization. A card catalog varied little from one library to another. Despite the basic method for creating a computerized catalog, the business of developing and marketing online catalogs became a competitive one. A large number of companies provide automated library systems today. One may learn to use the online catalog in one particular library and find that a similar tool in another library works very differently. The same information is contained, but the method for retrieving it is not the same. Successful efforts have been made to move toward a time when every automated library system is very easy for the user to operate.

In most of today's libraries there are computer terminals or microcomputers which allow access to the online library catalog for that institution. Most of the original library systems were large mainframe computer systems. Library users used "dumb" mainframe terminals to search the catalogs. Newer technology has allowed the library systems to be contained on smaller computers and accessed via individual microcomputer work stations. The microcomputer work stations of newer library systems allow the user to access the online catalog of the particular library as well as to do other computing tasks. Some systems operate in a Windows-based environment and others are accessed via the World Wide Web. Future work stations will enable the library user to sit down at one microcomputer and search for materials in the library catalog, to access CD-ROM indexes to which the library subscribes, to connect to the Internet and search globally for information on a topic, and to connect to remote databases that retrieve the actual text of publications. The user will be able to retrieve information and edit it into his or her own word processor as needed to produce notes, research papers, speeches, or whatever may be desired.

Author or Title Searches

Most online systems in libraries can be searched by the author's name or the title. These searches are the easiest to do. It is only when you have a very common name to search such as Robert Jones, or you can remember only bits of a title, that these kinds of searches may be difficult. Most often, when searching for an author's works, the last name is entered first, followed by the first name or initials, if known. A sample author search in an online catalog is shown in Figure 3.5.

The search typed in was "a=king martin luther." The screen in Figure 3.5 shows the first ten entries of the eleven found. Some are books and some are visuals, probably videos. Also notice that the first entry — number 1 — is not for a book, but rather lets the user know that the complete author heading is *King Martin Luther Jr. 1929-1968*. On this system, If you desire to look at one of the records for any of the entries indicated you would type the line number and press enter. If you wanted to view entry number 11 you could type FOR (or just the letter F) to go forward to the next screen.

Figure 3.5

```
Search Request: A=KING MARTIN LUTHER      LUIS Combined Catalog
Search Results: 11 Entries Found                    Author Index

-----------------------------------------------------------------
KING MARTIN LUTHER
     1    *Search Under: KING MARTIN LUTHER JR 1929-1968

          KING MARTIN LUTHER 1899-1984
     2    DADDY KING AN AUTOBIOGRAPHY <1980>

          KING MARTIN LUTHER JR 1929-1968
     3    GREAT SPEECHES VOLUME I <1985> visual
     4    SEARCH FOR THE BELOVED COMMUNITY THE THINKING <1986>
     5    STRENGTH TO LOVE <1963>
     6    STRIDE TOWARD FREEDOM THE MONTGOMERY STORY <1958>
     7    TESTAMENT OF HOPE THE ESSENTIAL WRITINGS OF <1986>
     8    TRUMPET OF CONSCIENCE <1968>
     9    WHERE DO WE GO FROM HERE CHAOS OR COMMUNITY <1967>
    10    WHY WE CANT WAIT <1964>
------------------------------------- CONTINUED on next page ----
STArt over      Type number to display record              <F8>
FORward page
HELp
OTHer options
Next Command:
```

Selecting entry number 6 will retrieve the screen shown in Figure 3.6. All the necessary information for identifying and retrieving this book is found in this record.

Title searching normally uses the exact words in the title of the work in their correct order. If the first

Figure 3.6

```
Search Request: A=KING MARTIN LUTHER       LUIS Combined Catalog
BOOK - Record 6 of 11 Entries Found                    Brief View
------------------------------------------------------------------
   Author:        King, Martin Luther, Jr., 1929-1968.
   Title:         Stride toward freedom; the Montgomery story.
   Edition:       <1st ed.>
   Published:     New York, Harper <1958>
   Subjects:      Segregation in transportation--Montgomery, Ala.
                  Afro-Americans--Alabama--Montgomery
                  Montgomery (Ala.)--Race question.
------------------------------------------------------------------
   LOCATION:               CALL NUMBER              STATUS:
   CIRCULATING (A-K 2nd   E185.89 T8 K5    Charged, Due 11/07/97
      / L-Z 3rd Flr)

   STArt over          LONg view            <F6> NEXt record
   HELp                INDex                <F5> PREvious record
    OTHer options

   NEXT COMMAND:
```

word is "a," "an," or "the," then it is omitted. When "a," "an," or "the" occurs *within* the title, it is included in the search. A sample search for a title is shown in the example illustration shown in Figure 3.7.

Figure 3.7

```
Search Request: T=GONE WITH THE WIND       LUIS Combined Catalog
Search Results: 4 Entries Found                        Title Index
------------------------------------------------------------------
   GONE WITH THE WIND
   1 <1985> visual
   2 MITCHELL MARGARET <1936>
   3 MITCHELL MARGARET <1964>
   4 MITCHELL MARGARET 1900-1949. GONE WITH THE WIND <1985>  visual

------------------------------------------------------------------
   STArt over          Type number to display record
   HELp
   OTHer options
   NEXT COMMAND:
```

Figure 3.8

```
Search Request: T=GONE WITH THE WIND     LUIS Combined Catalog
BOOK - Record 3 of 4 Entries Found              Brief View
-------------------------------------------------------------------
Author:         Mitchell, Margaret, 1900-1949.

Title:          Gone with the wind
Edition:        <Book club ed.>

Published:      New York : Macmillan, c1964.

Subjects:       United States--History--Civil War, 1861-1865--Fiction.
-------------------------------------------------------------------
  LOCATION:               CALL NUMBER           STATUS:
  CIRCULATING (A-K 2nd    PZ3 M69484 go7        Not checked out
  / L-Z 3rd Flr
---------------------------------------------------- Page 1 of 1 --
STArt over          LONg view                <F6> NEXt record
HELp                INDex                     <F5> PREvious record
OTHer options

NEXT COMMAND:
```

The title being searched is *Gone With the Wind*. The third word is the article "the," but since it is not the first word of the title, it is used. Four records were located; two are books and two are visuals, probably videos. (Remember that the online catalog may include all materials housed in the library, not just books.)

Choosing number 3 from the four choices offered in the above example will lead to the record with information about that item as shown in Figure 3.8. Again, all the pertinent information that you need to identify and locate this book can be found in this "Brief View" of this record. All you really need to write down is the call number — PZ3 M6984 go7— go to the correct floor, take it off the shelf and check it out at the Circulation desk.

Subject Searching

Using a library's online catalog to search for materials by subject requires the user to understand the concept of *subject headings*. When attempting to group library materials together according to the similarity of their subject matter, it is important to create a system which controls the words selected as subject headings. This standardization allows libraries to be fairly certain that a user can search for materials using the same terms from one library to the next. A standard system of controlled subject headings led to the notion of cross references from one similar subject heading to another similar or related heading.

In most academic libraries, the *Library of Congress Subject Headings* is the listing used for subject access to materials. Currently a four volume set of books, the *Library of Congress Subject Headings* is a good place to start when looking for information in a library. Consult this alphabetic listing to determine

Figure 3.9

```
Search Request: S=SECOND LANGUAGE ACQUISITION  LUIS Combined Catalog
Search Results: 55 Entries Found                              Subject
Guide
  ----------------------------------------------------------------
LINE:    BEGINNING ENTRY:                           INDEX RANGE:
1        SECOND LANGUAGE ACQUISITION                        1-19
2        SECOND LANGUAGE ACQUISITION                       20-38
3        SECOND LANGUAGE ACQUISITION                       39-55
  ----------------------------------------------------------------
STArt over       Type number to begin display within index range
HELp
OTHer options

NEXT COMMAND:
```

appropriate subject headings to use in the online catalog. Try to think of synonymous words for the topic you are looking for in order to determine the most closely related headings (See Figure 3.1 for sample of broad LC subject headings).

Subject searching (the S= command in the examples shown) requires the use of the subject headings that have been assigned to a work. The searcher may refer to the *Library of Congress Subject Headings* to determine a subject heading to search. A sample subject heading is **second language acquisition**. A

Figure 3.10

```
Search Request: S=SECOND LANGUAGE ACQUISITION
                                      LUIS Combined Catalog
Search Results: 55 Entries Found            Subject Index
  -----------------------------------------------------------------
* Heading Continued from Prior Page --------- Page BACK to View
     SECOND LANGUAGE ACQUISITION
    20   INSTRUCTED SECOND LANGUAGE ACQUISITION LEARN      <1990>
    21   INTERACTIVE APPROACHES TO SECOND LANGUAGE RE      <1988>
    22   INTERLANGUAGE PHONOLOGY THE ACQUISITION OF A      <1987>
    23   ISSUES IN SECOND LANGUAGE ACQUISITION MULTIP      <1988>
    24   LANGUAGE ANXIETY FROM THEORY AND RESEARCH TO      <1991>
    25   LANGUAGE TRANSFER IN LANGUAGE LEARNING            <1994>
    26   LEARNING STRATEGIES IN SECOND LANGUAGE ACQUI      <1990>
    27   LINGUISTIC PERSPECTIVES ON SECOND LANGUAGE A      <1989>
    28   MAKING IT HAPPEN INTERACTION IN THE SECOND L      <1988>
    29   READING FOR MEANING AN INTEGRATED APPROACH T      <1991>
    30   ROLE OF THE FIRST LANGUAGE IN FOREIGN LANGUA      <1987>
    31   SECOND LANGUAGE ACQUISITION FOREIGN LANGUAGE      <1990>
    32   SECOND LANGUAGE CLASSROOMS RESEARCH ON TEACH      <1988>
  -------------------------- CONTINUED on next page ----
STArt over          Type number to display record  <F8> FORward page
HELp                GUIde                           <F7> BACk page
OTHer options
NEXT COMMAND:
```

subject search will locate all materials in the catalog which have been assigned that subject heading. Searching for the subject **second language acquisition** results in the screen example in Figure 3.9.

Selecting item number 2 from the choices retrieves the screen in Figure 3.10. As you can see, this is a screen that shows a listing of titles beginning with number 20, which is what the **Index Range** in Figure 3.9 indicates.

Notice at the bottom of the screen the various commands that you can use to either **start** all over with a beginning screen, go **forward** one page (or screen), go back to the **guide**, receive **help**, or bring up a list of other **options** available to you. You do not have to return to the initial search screen to begin a new search. At the bottom of the screen is the **Next Command:** line. You can initiate a new search right here. Just type in the command for the type of search you want to do: a=, t=, s=, k=, etc., enter the data, and press enter.

Retrieving item number 23 leads to the screen as illustrated in Figure 3.11. This is the record for the book, *Issues in Second Language Acquisition: Multiple Perspectives.*

Figure 3.11

```
Search Request: S=SECOND LANGUAGE ACQUISITION    LUIS Combined Catalog
BOOK - Record 23 of 55 Entries Found                     Brief View
   --------------------------------------------------------------------
Title:          Issues in second language acquisition : multiple
                perspectives
Published:      New York : Newbury House Publishers, c1988.
Subjects:       Second language acquisition.
   --------------------------------------------------------------------
LOCATION:            CALL NUMBER            STATUS:
RESERVES             P118.2 I87 1988        Not checked out
(Closed Stacks)
(Restricted Access)


   --------------------------------------------- Page 1 of 1  --------
STArt over        LONg view                       <F6>NEXt record
HELp              INDex                            <F5>PREvious record
OTHer options     GUIde
NEXT COMMAND:
```

When looking at an item record, study the screen carefully. It will provide a lot of information about the item.

❖ You are looking at a Brief View of the record. To get more information than you see, type "LON," as indicated at the bottom of the screen, and press enter.

❖ The book is not in the circulating stacks. It is at Reserves and you must go there to ask for it.

❖ The call number is P118.2 87 1988.

❖ This book is not checked out.

Keyword Searching

In most electronic catalogs there is a method by which any keyword may be searched to locate information. A keyword is any word that the system indexes. It can be a subject word, a word in a title, an author's name, or other term that the system has been designed to index. The computer record sometimes contains other information that can be keyword searched. There may be a listing of chapters within a book or a short annotation of the item. Keywords from these annotations or chapter listings can retrieve useful books and materials.

Keywords in electronic databases frequently can be combined using Boolean logic ("and" "or" "not," see Chapter 5 for a more complete description). This allows the user to combine two or more terms, to search phrases, or to combine a search for an author's name with words from a title. Depending upon the system, the keyword search capabilities may be very sophisticated. Following are some examples of Boolean searches:

solar energy and automobiles
(solar energy or methane) and automobiles

These two searches find materials about alternative fuels.

Note the use of the parentheses to show which terms are synonymous. A library's online catalog may use this method for organizing the search strategy or it may use another. Most electronic catalogs will have some online assistance available through HELP keys or commands. Frequently one can learn how to use a system without assistance from anyone, but whenever in doubt, seek out the employees at the library's reference desk for assistance.

Many online systems allow searches for specific call numbers, as well as searching for terms in specific fields — author, title, subject, etc. Depending upon the knowledge you have regarding what you want to locate, you may choose a variety of different methods to search for information in an online catalog. Some practice will usually be needed any time you enter an unfamiliar library in order to acquaint yourself with the system at use in that library. The important thing to remember is that the principal key for locating information by author, title, subject or keyword is available in virtually any online system you may encounter. Only the keystrokes for performing the search may vary from system to system.

THINK ABOUT THIS....

Locating one record for a book, video, etc., dealing with the subject your are interested in will give you leads to other works about the same subject. Looking at the subject headings indicated in a record will give you an insight to the way librarians catalog items about the same subject. One "good hit" is like discovering an entire gold mine.

Developments

All library online catalogs are designed to do the same thing: to inform the user of library holdings and indicate where they are located. Different libraries employ different computer systems for providing this service. A recent development is toward online catalogs with graphical interfaces. They combine the power of online searching with the ease of point-and-click navigation.

Another development to look for is standardization among catalogs. In the past, a library's card catalog was available only inside the walls of that library building. Today technology allows the user to access library online catalogs from remote sites. They may operate over the Internet via the World Wide Web, telnet, or gopher. Other catalogs may be accessed by direct dial through a modem. Different libraries use different computer systems for their online catalogs. Communication standards, such as those set down in ANSI Z39.50, encourage all computer systems to "speak the same language." Now it is possible to search many library catalogs while sitting at a single computer.

The changes and improvements to online access to library catalogs will continue. The goal of quicker and easier access to information will mandate further change.

CASE IN POINT

Elaine, a student, needs to research how color (such as in clothing and room color) affects a person's mood. She does not know any authors or titles for books on this subject. She has tried to locate a subject heading in the *LC Subject Headings Guide*, but has not been successful. Therefore, she decides to perform a keyword search to see if she can come up with a book on her topic. Then she can see what subject headings are used in that record to describe that book. A good keyword search to start is "color and behavior." If that doesn't work she could try other combinations and synonyms for these keywords, such as "color and mood."

PAPER INDEXES

The words "journal," "magazine," "serial," and "periodical" are all words that refer to a publication that is issued at regular intervals, such as weekly, monthly, quarterly, semiannually, etc., and continue for an indefinite period of time. The term "periodical" is a generic term which includes magazines, journals, newspapers, newsletters, bulletins, etc. "Magazine" is usually applied to more popular titles, and "journal" is usually given to more scholarly titles.

One characteristic of a periodical is that each issue contains a number of articles by various authors. A periodical usually provides the same type of information from issue to issue. *Time* magazine has always provided non-technical articles on current events while *Journal of Abnormal Psychology* provides long scholarly articles about abnormal psychology.

A periodical differs from a book in that it is often more current. A periodical that is issued every month will have newer information than a book that is updated once every year or once every decade. A periodical is usually more specialized in its treatment of a subject. For these reasons, periodicals can be an excellent source of information for research projects.

Periodical Indexes

Basically there are three ways to locate periodical articles about a particular subject. First, and it is not recommended, students could begin browsing through as many periodicals as they can find, trying to "luck" into what they need. Second, if a student knows what periodical publishes articles on certain subjects, he or she could search through the index to that periodical. *(Some* periodicals, especially those considered scholarly journals, have a self-index at the end of each year or volume.) Third, the easiest and most efficient way to find a periodical article is to use a periodical index.

Periodical indexes provide access to articles by subject and sometimes also by author or title. They are issued at frequent intervals and are often cumulated annually. Indexes mainly provide a document citation, that is the information needed to go find the desired item in a library. A book citation, for instance, includes the title of the publication, the author, name of publisher, and place and date of publication. A journal article citation includes the title and author of an article, the title of the magazine or journal, and the volume and page number of the issue. Some indexing tools also include a short summary of every article. They are often referred to as "abstracts," such as *Psychological Abstracts*.

An index can be general in nature, covering almost every subject under the sun, such as the popular *Readers' Guide to Periodical Literature. Readers' Guide* has been published since 1900. It covers all kinds of general interest subjects in over 150 popular U.S. magazines. *Reader's Guide* does not index scholarly journals. An index can also be highly specialized, covering specific subject fields such as *Art Index, Education Index,* or *Animal Breeders' Abstracts.* Subject-specific indexes and abstracts will be covered in the last three chapters of this book.

Prefatory Pages

Unless you have a full understanding of the particular index you are about to use, it is best to start at the beginning. Look at the prefatory pages located at the beginning of any of the volumes to find important information on how to use the index. When students use periodical indexes, usually their most frequent questions are about how to read all the abbreviations and numbers. The prefatory pages will clear up any confusion a user might have.

Most prefatory pages include a table of abbreviations of periodical titles. Periodical titles are often abbreviated in order to save space in the entries. Also, there is usually a listing of all the periodicals indexed with pertinent information such as subscription cost, publication frequency, and publisher. A third part of the prefatory pages is the collection of abbreviations used in the index, including abbreviations for months of the year, illustrations, etc. The last and probably most important part of the prefatory section is a *sample entry* that identifies all the parts of the bibliographic citation. These four components of the prefatory pages are illustrated in the following examples.

Figure 4.1 is a short example of abbreviations used in periodical titles.

Figure 4.1

```
     Abbreviations of Periodicals Indexed

                 A                   Black Enterp - Black Enterprise
Aging - Aging
                                     BYTE - BYTE
Am Herit - American Heritage
                                                 C
Art News - Art News

Aviat Week Space Technol - Avia-    Car Driv - Car and Driver
tion Week & Space Technology
                                     Change - Change
                 B                   Consum Rep - Consumer Reports

Better Homes Gard - Better Homes
and Gardens

BioScience - BioScience
```

Figure 4.2 is an example of an abbreviations table.

Figure 4.2

Abbreviations

+	= continued on later pages of same issue		Mr	= March
Ag	= August		My	= May
Ap	= April		N	= November
Aut	= Autumn		no	= number(s)
bibl	= bibliography		O	= October
Dept	= Department		S	= September
ed	= edition, editor		Spr	= Spring
il	= illustrations,-s		Summ	= Summer
Je	= June		Wint	= Winter
Jl	= July		yr	= year

Figure 4.3 is a sample entry with important sections labeled. The citation contains all the necessary information for locating the specific article. Explanations for each label are below.

See Also Reference -- leads you to related subject headings and other like terms. Sometimes *See Also* references are more narrowly focused than the subject heading offered.

See Reference -- Indicates that this term/concept is not a subject heading used in this index and it offers the correct subject heading.

Subject Heading -- This article is about dieting. Subject headings are identified by their bold face type. Notice that this is a true subject heading, not an author heading. However when an author is used as a heading, his name is not repeated (see Figure 4.4). For every author heading there will be at least one subject heading for that same article.

Article Title -- Title of this specific article.

Author -- This is the author of this article.

Journal Title -- Name of the journal where this article appears.

Illustrations -- This article is illustrated.

Volume Number -- The volume of this particular issue is 202

Paging -- This article is found on pages 33 through 36, and continued on later pages in this same issue.

Date of Journal -- This journal was issued on May 19, 1996.

Figure 4.3

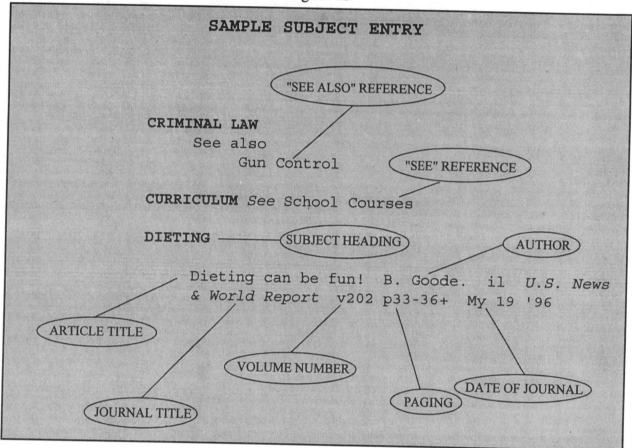

Another type of entry is a person's name. The name entry is used when a person is the subject or an author of an article. Figure 4.4 shows both types of entries. The first citation is an article written *by* Tom Watson. The second is an article *about* Tom Watson. Notice that the second entry is separated by the word "about." The subject heading "Watson, Tom" is used for both entries.

Figure 4.5 is an example of the information offered in the section of the *Readers' Guide* reflecting the various periodicals indexed. Notice that more than just the title is given. Along with the title is the price, frequency of issuance, ISSN, name of the publisher, and the address of the publisher.

Figure 4.4

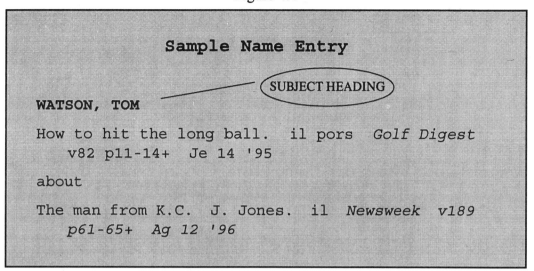

Uniformity of Indexes

As you work with paper indexes, you will discover that the different indexes have a lot in common.   For example, as was shown in the Figure 4.4, subject headings often are in boldface type. Whether the entry is a subject or an author's name, the boldface headings are arranged alphabetically. For every author entry there will be at least one subject heading for that same article. When a person's name serves as the heading, the articles written *by* that person will be listed first, followed by the word "about" in italics, to point out that the remaining entries are written *about* that person by another. After the headings, the entries are listed in alphabetical order and indented for easy identification. Therefore, it is easy to identify each entry's article title, author, periodical title, volume number, issue number, pages and date.

Main headings can also have subheadings to further divide the entries into more specialized subject divisions. The subheadings are also in boldface type; however, they are not in all capital letters. Cross-references, *See* and *See Also*, are given to direct the user to one or more synonyms. A "SEE" reference will show what term(s) are used *instead* of the one you used. For instance, "capital punishment" may be the preferred term *instead* of "death penalty." A *See Also* cross-reference will be given if additional entries are available to augment the one found. For instance, in addition to looking up articles about alcoholism, such terms as "substance abuse" and "addiction" could *also* be used.

Search Strategy

Searching indexes is similar to searching the card catalog or online catalog. The same strategies can be used. The first step is to have a subject in mind. This includes selecting various terms that describe the subject and are included in the controlled vocabulary (such as those that appear in *Library of Congress Subject Headings* or *Thesaurus of ERIC Descriptors*.) Second, determine which indexes will most likely cover the subject you have chosen and, starting with the most recent issue, begin looking for that subject heading(s). Third, after locating the entries you want, copy all the bibliographic information (article title, author, name of the periodical, volume, pages, issue date), remembering that this information will be useful in locating that exact article. Next, determine if the library

Figure 4.5

```
            Periodicals Indexed


                   A

Ad Astra. $35. bi-m (ISSN 1041-        (ISSN 0006-0151) Better
  102X) National Space Soci-         Homes and Gardens, P.O. Box
  ety. 922 Pennsylvania Ave.,        55211, Boulder, CO 80322-
  SE, Washington, DC 20003-          5211
  2140
                                     Bicycling. $19.97. 11 times a
Aging. $6.50. q (ISSN 0002-0966)       yr (ISSN 0006-2073) Rodale
  Superintendent of Documents,         Press, Inc., 33 E. Minor St.,
  U.S. Government Printing Of-         Emmaus, PA 18098
  fice, Washington, DC 20402
  Ceased publication with No.        BioScience. $193. m (bi-m Jl/
  366, 1994                            Ag) (ISSN 0006-3568)
                                       BioScience Circulation.
American History. $23.95. bi-m         AIBS, 730 11th St. N.W.,
  (ISSN 1076-8866) American          Washington DC 20001-4521
  History, P.O. Box 8200, Har-
  risburg, PA 17105-8200 For-
  merly American History Il-                     C
  lustrated; name changed with
  June 1994                          Canada and the World. $21
                                       m (S-My) (ISSN 0043-8170)
Artnews.  See Art News               Canada and the World, Box
                                       22099, Westmount Postal
Aviation Week & Space Technol-         Outlet, Waterloo, Ont. N2L
  ogy. $105 w (ISSN 0005-2175)         6J7, Canada Continued by:
  Aviation Week & Space Tech-          Canada and the World
  nology, P.O. Box 503,                Backgrounder
  Hightstown, NJ 08520-9899          Car and Driver. $19.94 m
                                       (ISSN 0008-6002) Car and
                                       Driver, P.O. Box 52906,
                   B                   Boulder, CO 80322-2906


Better Homes and Gardens. $17 m
```

you are using owns or has access to that source. Finally, locate the source and find the article you need.

Libraries will have some tool (card catalog, computer printout, or online catalog) that will advise what newspaper, magazines, or journals, etc. they own or have access to. This "holdings list" will usually indicate other valuable information, such as beginning and ending date of subscription, whether the title is on microform, and where it is located in the library.

Newspapers

Newspapers are as much a research tool as books or periodicals, and they existed a long time before periodicals became a major media source. National or major newspapers are comprehensive, generally objective, and report the national and international news with authority. These include *USA Today*, *The New York Times*, and *Wall Street Journal*. *New York Times* and *Wall Street Journal* also happen to be self-indexed. Local newspapers may give a superficial report of major national or international events but can provide in-depth information on local happenings.

New York Times Index. (1913-). New York: Times.

As with many daily newspapers, *The New York Times* condenses the major happenings around the world, presenting history on a day-by-day basis. It covers all subjects that are newsworthy and even prints word-for-word some statements and speeches. The *Times* also contains several subject sections, such as the business and sports news, obituaries of famous people around the world, and a review section for books, movies, or plays. Most importantly for researchers, the *Times* began publication in 1851. Indexing is available from the very first issue.

In order to locate any piece of information within the mountain of written words printed in *The New York Times*, its index must be used. However, each volume of the *Index* covers a precise period of time. The *New York Times Index* is issued twice a month, with quarterly and annual cumulations. Therefore, if you want to locate a particular event, you must know the date (year) of that happening. For example, for a report of the Kennedy assassination that was written just after it happened, it is necessary to know that the assassination occurred in 1963. (Keep in mind that articles may continue to be written about an event or happening long after it has taken place.) If the event was within the last year, the month the event happened is needed in order to locate the correct semi-monthly issue or quarterly cumulation.

The information provided in the index consists of boldface type subject headings arranged in alphabetical order, with subheading in italics occasionally preceded by a black dot (bullet) ●. The headings are very specific and describe the most important aspect (person or event) of the entry. Related materials are sometimes collected under one common heading. A heading with multiple words can be inverted so that the most identifying word is at the beginning. For example, Walker, Stephen (last name first); or Cognitive Studies, Institute (instead of beginning with the word Institute.) Except in listings under book reviews, deaths, or theatre reviews, etc., the entries under each subject will be in chronological

Figure 4.6

FIREARMS. See also
Motion Pictures, N 5
Robberies and Thefts, N 8

Many states eagerly emulate Florida law allowing people without serious criminal records to carry concealed weapons, but studies by University of Maryland and Violence Policy Center show that Florida's gun law has allowed felons to obtain guns legally and that weapons have been linked to increase in killings in some cities (M), N 2,A,16:4

Two major gun promoters in Texas decide that state law allowing people to carry concealed weapons after Jan 1 is not a good idea for their gun shows; say they would ban concealed guns at their events (S), N 10,A,24:2

order, from January to December. Entries are arranged in paragraphs that provide the significant information (who, what, why, when, or where) about that particular article. They will also tell if the article is accompanied by a photograph, document, map, cartoon, or other material. Each entry provides bibliographic information, such as section, date, page, and column.

The length of the article is also given in the entry. There are three indicators for this: (L) for long articles over 2 columns; (M) for medium articles up to 2 columns; and (S) for an item of less than half a column. Cross-references are used when necessary. Cross-references guide the user to more specific headings and may give the date of the entry. Cross-reference terms that are used include: *See Also*, which directs the user to headings where related articles are located; and *Use*, which shows what term(s) is used instead of that heading. Figure 4.6 is an example of an entry from a newspaper index, November 1995, with an explanation of the parts.

If we had first looked up the term "Guns," we would have been directed to "Use Firearms." In the above entries, "Firearms" is the subject heading. The two entries shown are arranged chronologically. The first article is between one-half column to two columns in length (M), while the second is less than half a column (S). The bibliographic information for the first article is November 2, section A, page 16, column 4. For the second it is November 10, section A, page 24, column 2. Note that the year is not provided. Since these entries were found in the November 1995 index, we know that these articles will be found in the November 2 and November 10, 1995, issues of the paper.

NewsBank electronic information system. [CD-ROM]. (1990-). New Canaan, CT: NewsBank.

NewsBank is an index to selected articles from more than 450 newspapers in the United States. It does not contain *all* articles in a specific newspaper and it does not contain advertisements or classified ads. Editors choose which articles will go into the database.

NewsBank is similar to the other indexes discussed in this chapter, except that

it is both an index and a full-text collection to many newspapers. From 1996 to the present, the NewsBank Index provides full-text searching of selected newspaper articles from 500 sources. For articles before 1996, a paper index provides the number to a piece of microfiche where each article can be read. The paper index provides four pieces of information needed to locate that article in the microfiche collection. These are the specific year of the index (Ex: 1987), the abbreviated microfiche category (Ex: "LAW & LEGAL SYSTEMS"), the microfiche card number within the category (Ex: 7), and the microfiche grid coordinates (Ex: D6-8).

Internet Resources

Chicago Tribune [Online]. Available: *http://www.chicago.tribune.com/*

Kansas City Star [Online]. Available: *http://www.kcstar.com/library/library.htm*
Search the entire paper from 1991 to the present, and retrieve the full-text of the articles.

The New York Times. [Online]. Available: *http://www.nytimes.com/ nytimes*
Contains recent, abbreviated news only.

USA Today. [Online]. Available: http://www.usatoday.com/

Note: These addresses are valid as of the publication date. Internet addresses, however, can change frequently.

CASE IN POINT

Your instructor in one of your classes has given you a topic for your term paper. The topic is, "Do Entitlement Programs like Welfare Encourage Continuing Dependence on the System?" To find library materials, you must decide which search tools to use. *Readers Guide to Periodical Literature* is good for finding magazine articles on current events. The next step is to decide which term to look up in the index. Since the main topic of the paper is "Welfare," that would be a good place to start. When looking up "Welfare" in *Readers Guide*, we are told to "see" the term "Public Welfare" instead. Under the heading "Public Welfare" is a long list of entries. When you find articles that may be appropriate for your paper, write down which magazines they are in, which issue, and which pages. The next step is to determine if the library subscribes to the magazine. If the library doesn't subscribe, you can get the article through Interlibrary Loan.

5 ELECTRONIC INDEXES

This chapter discusses general electronic indexes and abstracting tools that one could use for library research. The term "electronic" refers to using a computer to complete the research process. This could be done using databases on CD-ROMs physically located in the library building or using a computer to connect to a remote database located in another state or even another country.

A variety of electronic databases are available to libraries. Most index magazine and/or journal articles. Others index research reports, books, or government documents. A few databases provide the full text of the articles right at the computer. Most, however, only provide the article citation, the information needed to find an article: author, article title, magazine name, volume number, date, etc. Librarians purchase the databases that will best help their clients and that they can afford to purchase.

There are several advantages to electronic searching.

A. Speed. A person can save hours or even days of research time using the computer. An electronic index can search several years' worth of articles at a time, while paper indexes usually cover one year or less per volume.

B. Thoroughness. The chances of missing important material or information is reduced by using the computer.

C. Flexibility. Boolean logic (using the terms "and" "or" "not") is used to give search instructions to a computer. This provides a way to combine or exclude terms. Good search instructions increase the accuracy and relevance of the search.

D. Electronic Format. Most databases allow the user to print or save search results to a diskette. Such data is easily inserted into word processing documents.

Electronic resources may not be for everyone, especially if a person feels he or she can manually obtain enough information in a relatively short period of time. Why? First, a library's best index for a particular subject may only be available in paper or book format. Second, there may be a charge for doing a computer search. The costs are based on the database cost, telephone costs, prints, and any surcharge. Databases vary in cost, depending on the company that is selling the service. Otherwise, there are few, if any, disadvantages in doing a computer search. And even if facilities for manual searching are available, a computer search may be the best means for locating the information you seek.

Boolean Logic

Boolean operators were invented by a British mathematician named George Boole. The symbolic language is used to express logical relationships. They provide a way to tell an electronic index exactly what information is needed. The three boolean operators used most often in electronic library searching are:

a. "OR" Logic. The computer searches a database for items with *any* one or more of the requested terms. For example, a search for *apples or oranges* will return every item that contains the word *apple* plus every item that contains the word *orange*. A few records, by coincidence, may even contain both terms. "Or" searches provide more records

b. " AND" Logic. The computer searches a database for those records that contain *all* the requested terms. For example, a search for *apples and oranges* will return every record that contains both concepts. "And" searches provide fewer records.

c. "NOT" Logic. The computer searches a database, then rejects those records that contain the unwanted term. Examples are *fruit not oranges*; or *pets not dogs*. The "not" command is used infrequently, as it can inadvertently exclude useful material.

As another example, a person may be searching for information on the death penalty for women in foreign countries. A simple search of "death penalty" in a magazine index may return a lot of information not wanted by the student. Such a broad search would return articles about the death penalty in the United States, and articles about men receiving the death penalty. Such a simple search may also leave out desirable articles. It may leave out article records described with the words "capital punishment" or "euthanasia." The student could try again with a more complex search, as diagrammed below:

death penalty or capital punishment or euthanasia	AND	women or females	NOT	United States

These concepts must be changed from regular English phrases to a format that a computer can understand. The search described above would be typed into some indexing databases as follows:

((death penalty or capital punishment or euthanasia) and (women or females)) not United States

This is quite a complex search. Once users understand the format the computer needs, it is relatively easy to set up a good computer search.

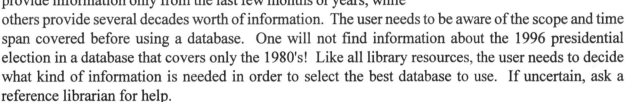

Electronic indexes are produced and sold to libraries by a number of companies. Each company's product uses different search software. This means they can look different and require different commands. Most electronic databases, however, have a number of features in common.

A. **Focus and scope of coverage**. Databases will focus on indexing a particular kind of information. Some databases index only business magazines. Others index only government documents. Some provide information only from the last few months or years, while others provide several decades worth of information. The user needs to be aware of the scope and time span covered before using a database. One will not find information about the 1996 presidential election in a database that covers only the 1980's! Like all library resources, the user needs to decide what kind of information is needed in order to select the best database to use. If uncertain, ask a reference librarian for help.

B. **Citations**. Most electronic databases provide only the document citation: author, title, date of publication, etc. It is up to the user to determine if the library owns or has access to the item found. Some databases also provide an abstract, or short summary of the item, although a few provide full text.

C. **Keyword searching**. Paper magazine indexes allow the user to search only by subject heading or author. The list of subject headings used in an index is controlled by the publisher, creating a "controlled vocabulary." Most electronic databases allow the user to search the database for a word or phrase *wherever* it appears in the citation. For instance, a search for the word "African" in a free-text search will return all citations that contain the word, whether it appears as a subject heading, a word in the title of an article, name of the periodical, or the article abstract. Occasionally the free-text search can backfire. If one was searching for articles *about* "John Smith," a free text search would also return every article written *by* somebody named John Smith. Keyword searching is sometimes called free-text searching.

D. **Field Searching**. Each item of a citation is contained in a "field." The author of an article is contained in the "author field," the title in the "title field." Every part of the citation, including an abstract if there is one, has a field. See Figure 5.1 for a typical citation. Notice how all the information is labelled with a field name. Most electronic databases allow searching by field. If one, for instance, were looking for articles *about* John Smith, the computer could be told to retrieve citations when the words "John" *and* "Smith" appear in the subject field.

E. **Boolean Logic**. Every database understands the three boolean operators of "and," "or," and "not." Subjects can be combined to create more complex and better targeted searches.

F. **Truncation.** Most electronic indexes allow the user to truncate a word with a symbol. If a word is truncated, the database will search for all possible suffixes for that word. For instance, if the term *govern?* is searched, the database will return all records with the word *govern, governor, government, governments, or governmental.* The question mark "?" is a common truncation symbol, as are the colon (:) and the pound sign (#).

G. **Print or Download**. Most electronic databases allow the user to either print the search results or download the information on the screen to a computer disk. There is usually a way to either

Figure 5.1

```
Access No:   02665134

Title:     Catching Kevin

Authors:   Shimomura, Tsutomu

Journal:   Wired   ISSN: 1059-1028
           Vol:4 Iss:2  Date: Feb 1996 p:119-123+
           Type: Feature  Length: Long  Illus: Illustration

Names:     Mitnick, Kevin; Shimomura, Tsutomu

Subjects:  Internet; Computer Crime; Fraud; Privacy

Abstract:  Superhacker Tsutomu Shimomura discusses how he tracked
           down computer criminal Kevin Mitnick and finally caught
           him.  Shimomura's chase illustrates well the thin
           veneer of privacy on the Internet.
```

download a single record or mark several to be downloaded in a batch.

H. Help. All electronic databases have help screens and/or printed help material available.

Remote Computer Searching

One method of using a computer to search for citations to articles, or possibly the entire article text, is connecting by World Wide Web or Telnet to a remote computer and accessing a database stored there. Such databases are rarely, if ever, free. Each college or university pays for access to online databases much in the same way they subscribe to paper magazines, newspapers, or CD-ROM magazine indexes.

Most college and university libraries have some capabilities to access a remote database for their users to complete research. One of the more common databases available to academic institutions is FirstSearch.

FirstSearch

FirstSearch is an online information system that provides access to a variety of databases. FirstSearch allows students, staff and faculty access to several databases beyond the confines of the library building. Searching the databases will provide citations to journal articles, books, conference proceedings, films, and more. It is then up to the user to take the citations and determine if the library

Internet Resources

World Wide Web Access to FirstSearch URL http://www.ref.oclc.org:2000/html/ fs_pswd.htm

has the materials or if they must request the materials through their local Interlibrary Loan Office.

FirstSearch is a product of OCLC (Online Computer Library Center, Inc.), a nonprofit organization which serves libraries and educational institutions. Each institution that subscribes to FirstSearch is issued a unique logon authorization and password. The construction of FirstSearch is user-friendly, allowing the user to access the system with little or no training. Online instructions are available for each basic step. FirstSearch presently offers 64 different databases. Some of the more popular ones are:

1. WorldCat   Books and other materials in 21,000 libraries worldwide.
2. Article1st   Index of articles from nearly 12,500 journals.
3. Contents1st   Table of contents of nearly 12,500 journals.
4. FastDoc   General magazine index of over 1,000 titles.
5. PapersFirst   An index of papers presented at conferences.
6. Proceedings   An index of conference publications.
7. ERIC   Journal articles and reports in education
8. GPO   U.S. Government publications, 1976-present.
9. MEDLINE   Abstracted articles from 3,500 medical journals.
10. NetFirst   Database of Internet-accessible resources.

All FirstSearch databases use the same search software. That means the same set of commands will work in all the databases. Like most electronic databases, it will accept author, title, subject, or keyword searches. Each database also has a list of additional search commands. For instance, the ERIC database can also be searched by institution name. The medical database MEDLINE can be searched by gene symbol or chemical substance. The search software will automatically conduct a keyword search unless another type of search is specifically requested.

to search by subject   *su:computers*
to search for two subjects   *su:computers and health*
to search by title   *ti:using computers to analyze DNA*
to search by author (use last name) *au:schmidt*

FirstSearch also supports the following functions:

Help Explains how to use the system.

Search Will begin another search.

Library Displays the libraries that own a given publication.

Limit Narrows the search strategy by year, type of document or language.

Email Orders displayed records to be sent to any email address. Up to five records at a time can be sent. For example, e 1-3, 7-8.

Database Choose another database to search.

Print To the printer attached to the computer.

EBSCO*host*

  EBSCO Information Services is a company that delivers a periodical index offered via the Internet. Like FirstSearch, it must be subscribed to by the institution. Each institution is given a particular Internet address to use. EBSCO*host* indexes thousands of magazines and journals. The database provides full text to many of the magazines and journals.

CARL Uncover

  Carl Uncover is one of the oldest online indexes available. The Uncover database presently indexes more than 20,000 magazines and journals in all subject areas. The database can presently be searched for free. The company will fax or mail the full-text of an article for a price.

Internet Resources

Carl Uncover. [Online]. Available: http://www.carl.org/unCover

CD-ROMS

  CD-ROM (Compact Disk - Read Only Memory) is a way to handle and transfer information much the same way as conducting a remote computer search. The differences are that one does not need to use the Internet to access the database, and usually there is no cost for the patron. Yet, you have the same capabilities with regard to using Boolean logic and in performing global or free-text searching in each database. Information for CD-ROM is stored on a compact disk measuring 4.7 inches in diameter. A single disk can hold as much information as 1,500 floppy disks, or approximately 250,000 pages of text. The most common library products available on CD-ROM are magazine and journal indexes. Some other databases on CD-ROM are full-text. Examples of these include dictionaries, encyclopedias, and other reference sources.

A special CD-ROM drive, hooked up to a PC, is needed along with special software to search and read the information. There is a variety of bibliographic and information databases available on CD-ROM. Many of the most heavily used magazine and journal indexes used in colleges and universities, such as *Readers' Guide to Periodical Literature*, *General Science Index*, *Business Periodicals Index*, *Psychological Abstracts*, *Dissertation Abstracts*, *ERIC* and others are available on CD-ROM.

Most academic libraries subscribe to a variety of CD-ROM databases. Some may be located on a CD-ROM Network. This means that more than one individual can access the same database at the same time. Some can only be loaded on individual computer stations and used by one person at a time.

ProQuest Periodical Abstracts

ProQuest is a common general periodical index in college and university libraries. It is produced by UMI in Ann Arbor, Michigan. For any subject Proquest is a good place to start. Not only does it cover the different subject areas on a limited basis, it also indexes current interest and popular news magazines such as *Time*, *Newsweek*, and *U.S. News and World Reports*. The ProQuest database is quite large, as it indexes several hundred magazines and journals and provides a short summary of every article indexed. Generally only one or two years of the index fits on a single CD-ROM. It may be necessary to switch CD-ROMs in order to search for older articles.

Proquest treats regular searches as keyword searches. It is possible, however, to specify fields

---

DATABASE SEARCHING TIPS

❖If your search retrieved too many records, use "and" to combine another term and narrow your search.

❖Check the databases "wordlist" or "index" to make sure you are using the best subject headings.

❖If your search retrieved too few records, use "or" to include synonymous terms, or use the truncation symbol to include alternate word endings.

❖When you have identified relevant articles, look at the other fields (especially the subject field) to select more search words and phrases to continue your searching.

❖Use field searching to narrow your search.

❖Read the computer screen carefully for additional help and hints for using the database.

to search for a specific subject heading, author, magazine title, etc. Boolean operators can also be used when typing in a search strategy. For example, if the search "computer and crime" were entered, the computer would show the number of "hits" (records that match the search command(s)) that include both the word "computer" and the word "crime."

The full record includes an access number, title of the article, author(s) of the article, name of the journal, names of individuals, subjects headings and a brief abstract (see Figure 5.1.) The word or words included in the search will be highlighted throughout the record. Arrow keys and pageup/ pagedown keys can be used to move through the records. Information for locating an article can be written down from the screen or can be downloaded to a disk.

As is common with electronic databases, function keys can be used to perform various tasks.

<F1>=Help   <F2>=Commands   <F3>=New Search   <F4>=Save/Download
<F6>=Indexes   <F7>=Display Records, <F8>=Thesaurus   <F9>=Mark Records
<F10>=Restart

This has been a general introduction to only one CD-ROM database. There are several other companies that produce a variety of CD-ROM products. Figures 5.2 through 5.5 show various ways of typing in the same search in different electronic databases. The commands for performing various functions will vary from database to database, as will the truncation symbols.

Figure 5.2

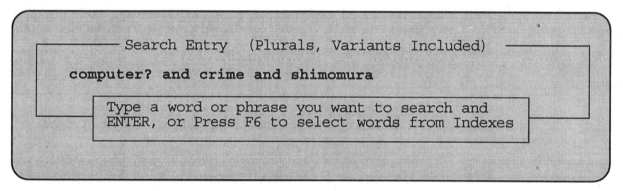

```
┌──────── Search Entry   (Plurals, Variants Included) ────────┐
│                                                              │
│  computer? and crime and shimomura                           │
│    ┌──────────────────────────────────────────────────┐     │
│    │ Type a word or phrase you want to search and       │     │
│    │ ENTER, or Press F6 to select words from Indexes     │     │
│    └──────────────────────────────────────────────────┘     │
└──────────────────────────────────────────────────────────────┘
```

Figure 5.3

Search For: su:computer+ and su:crime and au:shimomura

Start Search   WordList   Advanced Search

Figure 5.4

```
Enter your local search request
Subject Words: computers:
   2nd Subject: crime
   3rd Subject:

Person's Name: shimomura
   Title Words:
```

Figure 5.5

```
To learn more about the database          press F3
To learn more about the retrieval system  press F1
to use the Thesaurus                       press F9
```

FIND: **computer* and crime and shimomura**

Type a search then press Enter. Use the INDEX (F5) to pick terms.

THINK ABOUT THIS...

Because different electronic journal indexes have different directions for using them, they can be confusing. Try to think of the indexes as being different makes and models of automobiles. For example, you normally drive a 1983 Camaro and are asked to drive your parents' new Mercedes. You know how to drive a car, but you are not familiar with this make and model. You know it has a transmission, windshield wipers, headlights, radio, signal lights, etc., but you are not sure how to activate them. This is the same for using different CD-ROM products. You can search using Boolean operators, by specific field, and by subject. Yet, the commands and features are somewhat different. Ask for help when you need it!

FINDING AND USING REFERENCE RESOURCES

An academic library is very complex. Its collection is designed to support all the classes taught at the university and satisfy the needs of faculty and administration. The number of resources available in the library can be overwhelming, making a research project seem more difficult than it really is. The Reference area of the library is usually the best place to start. The reference collection is the center of the library collection. It will either provide the information needed or lead the user to where the information can be found.

Every library has a reference collection of books, serials, and electronic tools. These items provide brief pieces of information or lead you to further resources. Their usefulness makes them the most used items in the library. Some items easily fit this description, such as encyclopedias, dictionaries, magazine indexes, and the online catalog. Other items are included in the reference collection because they are useful, timely, or otherwise in high demand. The *Guinness Book of World Records* is a reference resource, as is the *Occupational Outlook Handbook*. What makes them both reference resources?

Reference resources often have features in common. Some characteristics that they often share:

Indexing	They are designed to be quickly consulted rather than read from front to back. Example: encyclopedias
Conciseness	They contain brief information to frequently asked questions. Example: dictionaries.
Timeliness	They are often updated frequently. Example: phone books.

Given this description, there is still much diversity among reference resources. They could be further divided into two types: direct tools and access tools. A direct tool simply provides the information needed. A dictionary, for instance, provides the correct spelling and pronunciation of a word. Access tools, on the other hand, *lead* to needed resources. The library catalog (explained in chapter 3) leads the user to books, videos, or other library-owned resources. It is continuously updated to reflect what the library owns. Similarly, magazine indexes lead the user to magazine or journal articles on a given subject. Major types of reference resources are:

Access Tools	Direct Tools	
Library online catalog (see Ch. 3)	Almanacs	Dictionaries
Indexes & Abstracts (see Chs. 4 & 5)	Atlases	Directories
	Bibliographies	Encyclopedias
	Biographical Works	Gazetteers
	Book Reviews	Handbooks/Manuals

Reference resources are usually located near the reference desk to be convenient to librarians and their clients. There are materials on all subjects, arranged by call number just like the circulating collection. Reference books do not circulate (they can not be checked out) so that the entire collection is always available to clients. They can be identified by the "Ref" notation above the call number:

Example:	Ref
	HT
	123
	C55

Occasionally, a few items in a library do not have a call number. The online catalog will indicate their location. Periodical indexes, phone books, and other such items may be located in prominent locations near the Reference Desk.

Below are listed some general resources in each category of reference sources. Most subject areas have their own, more specialized resources which are extremely useful for college students. Whatever your major, there are specialized dictionaries, encyclopedias, and other resources to help you with your coursework. These specialized resources are covered in the last four chapters of this book.

Almanacs

An almanac is a quick reference source for statistics and other information. They include answers to frequently requested information on a wide array of topics. Almanacs are used by anyone in need of general information, and are often the first resource consulted by librarians. Most almanacs are published annually (mainly updating the same body of material each year).

A general almanac includes such information as statistics for population characteristics, manufacturing yields, taxes, sports, and education. They often provide lists of award recipients, major cities, countries, famous people, natural disasters, and others subjects too numerous to mention. The several almanacs available are produced by different publishers and are therefore all slightly different in content. If you don't find your answer in one almanac, try another.

Information please almanac, atlas and yearbook. (1947-). New York: McGraw-Hill, Annual.

> Arranged by broad subject categories, with a detailed index at the beginning. Each issue also contains articles of current interest, such as environmental problems and consumer affairs.

Statistical abstract of the United States. (1878-). Washington, DC: G.P.O., Annual.

> This almanac is issued annually from the federal government. It is so useful that most librarians keep a copy handy at the library reference desk. It contains a spectrum of statistics compiled from the many government departments and some private organizations. The related *Historical Statistics of the United States, Colonial Times to 1970* provides historical information.

The world almanac and book of facts. (1868-). New York: Press Publishing, Annual.

> This work is what most people think of when they hear the word "almanac." This indispensable resource provides statistics and lists on a variety of topics. It also has some maps and pictures of the flags of the world. The information is arranged into broad subjects, but is best accessed from the detailed index at the beginning.

There are lots of almanacs available on special subjects. They can be very helpful for writing papers. They will provide statistics and other facts. Some include:

Adams resume almanac.

The African-American almanac.

County and city data book.

Digest of education statistics.

The information please environmental almanac.

The older Americans almanac: A reference work on seniors in the United States.

Places rated almanac: Your guide to finding the best place to live in America.

Sourcebook of criminal justice statistics.

CASE IN POINT

A student needs to know what percentage of the workforce was female from 1900 to the present. Since this is statistical information, almanacs are the ideal place to start. This type of information is gathered by the federal government, so an excellent choice is the *Statistical Abstract of the United States*. It provides labor force information for the last few years. Back issues will contain older numbers. The oldest numbers can be found in the related reference work, *Historical Statistics of the United States, Colonial Times to 1970*.

Atlases

An atlas is a reference work consisting largely of maps. The great advantage of an atlas is that maps are able to present complex information about an area in a manner that is easy to understand. As they say, "A picture is worth a thousand words." Most people think of an atlas when they are looking for a particular city, river, mountain range, country, or other physical representation. An atlas, however, can also show maps and tables of language, industry, natural resources, climate, culture, or even outer space. There are atlases available specifically for a states, countries, and the entire world.

Atlas of the United States. (1986). New York: Macmillan.

Britannica atlas. (1992). Chicago: Encyclopedia Britannica.

These are two traditional atlases showing physical features such as cities, roads, and political boundaries.

Dorling Kindersley world reference atlas. (1994). New York: Dorling Kindersley.

This atlas provides more in the way of information about countries and the world than detailed maps. It is often difficult to find worldwide statistics on crime, education, health, and wealth, but this atlas compares all countries on such standards in easy to read colorful charts.

Mattson, M. (1992). *Atlas of the 1990 census.* New York: Macmillan.

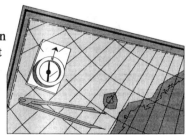

> The U.S. decennial census collects a large array of statistics on the American population. In this atlas the information is presented in easy to read maps. It includes country maps, regional maps, and state maps on such statistics as population by gender, age, and race. It also contains some housing information such as housing values by county and major city.

Rand McNally commercial atlas and marketing guide. (1878-). Chicago: Rand McNally, Annual.

> This atlas provides maps of each state depicting various economic and social features, such as educational institutions, population, business, manufacturers, and agriculture. Since it is reissued annually, the information can be counted on to be up-to-date.

Many other atlases exist that will provide specialized information. Some include:

Atlas of Florida

Atlas of world history.

Disease and medical care in the United States: A medical atlas of the twentieth century.

Bibliographies

A bibliography lists materials on a subject. In essence, it is a list of books, periodical articles, films, or other materials about a subject (such as seat belt safety or the Korean Conflict) or a person (such as William Shakespeare or Woodrow Wilson). Short bibliographies are a common sight at the end of journal articles and book chapters. Bibliographies in the Reference area and the circulating collection are entire books of such references. These bibliographies are used for conducting in-depth research on a topic. Book bibliographies can be found using the online catalog. There are also bibliographies of bibliographies. They serve as an index with headings for subjects and people. A major one is:

Bibliographic index: A cumulative bibliography of bibliographies. (1938-). New York: H.W. Wilson.

> Consult this index to find bibliographies on a subject. It indexes both book-size bibliographies and bibliographies in magazine and journal articles. It cumulates into annual volumes.

Biographical Information

Students very often come to the library needing information about a famous person. Libraries carry a large number of resources that provide biographical information. They range from directories providing basic facts to long encyclopedia-style columns. Biographical resources can be universal in scope or limited by geographical area, such as *Who's Who in America*, or by subject, such as *Outstanding Women Athletes, Leaders in Education, Baker's Biographical Dictionary of Musicians*, etc. Some only contain information about people presently alive, while others specialize in historical figures. A biographical reference work can be a bibliography or index as well. Below are examples of both kinds.

Note: It is possible that information about a person can vary from source to source. Many resources get their information directly from the person, relying sometimes on the person's memory. Other resources will sometimes check the information through other resources. It is helpful sometimes to double check important points with a second source.

Bio-Base. (1978-). Detroit: Gale Research, Annual.

> This is the number one stop for finding biographical information. *BIO-BASE* is actually an indirect resource. It indexes dozens and dozens of biographical resources. People's names are arranged alphabetically by last name. There will be an entry for every time a person is profiled in a resource. A very famous person could have over a hundred entries. Each entry refers to a resource by an abbreviated symbol. For instance, WW 83 = *Who's Who in America*, 1983 edition. A separate guide lists all the abbreviations and the location of the resource.

Biography index. (1946-). New York: H.W. Wilson, Annual.

> This comprehensive guide is also an indirect resource. It indexes periodicals, books, obituaries, diaries, and bibliographies that contain information about people. Entries are arranged alphabetically by name. A profession/occupation section is located in the back.

Current biography. (1940-). New York: H.W. Wilson, Annual.

> This is probably the most popular biographical reference tool of prominent people. Each annual cumulation adds more than 300 new personalities each year. The scope is international, but the people included are ones having some influence on American happenings. Each article is accompanied by a picture and will include a two to three page article along with a list of reference sources used to write it. The article heading includes name pronunciation (if needed), date of birth, and occupation. Each new volume only adds living people, but libraries keep all the old volumes to have everyone profiled since 1940.

McGraw-Hill encyclopedia of world biography (Vols 1-12). (1973). New York: McGraw-Hill.

> This resource is called a "retrospective biographical dictionary" because it contains entries on historical figures. Its profiles range from King Tut to Frank Sinatra. Each long article contains a portrait whenever possible and a list of citations for "Further Reading."

CASE IN POINT

In one of your classes you are asked to locate information about either Thomas Crapper or Charles Richard Drew and make a three page report and presentation in class. The first resource that should come to mind is BIO-BASE. Here you could determine where information exists from the many biographical sources available. The next step is to locate the sources and take notes. In your bibliography, you would not list BIO-BASE, but the sources you found using it. Bio-Base is a finding tool, like the online catalog and periodical indexes.

By The Way...Thomas Crapper was a noted British engineer who invented the flush toilet. Charles Richard Drew was a surgeon who was a pioneer in the preservation of blood plasma and directed the blood plasma programs for the U.S. and Great Britain during World War II. Drew died shortly after a car accident, bleeding to death. Some sources say that he was denied access to a nearby hospital because he was African-American.

Who's who in America. (1899-). Chicago: Marquis, Annual.

> This annual publication profiles almost 80,000 people who are notable enough to meet the publisher's "Standards of Admission." It provides a short entry containing such information as birthday, education, position, and major achievements. When a person dies they are removed from the next edition. For that reason, libraries keep their older editions for reference to deceased persons. Marquis also publishes an international version called *Who's who in the world.*

Book Reviews

Most newly published books are reviewed by scholars and journalists. These reviews, published in magazines and newspapers, are valuable to college students. Like movie reviews, they help students decide whether or not to invest their time. This can be very helpful information before selecting a book to read for a book report! Book reviews can be found using some periodical indexes and the two resources below. Reviews are usually published between several months to a year after the book was published.

Book review digest. (1905-). New York: H.W. Wilson, Annual.

> Reviews of books are gathered from over 50 magazines and arranged under the author's last name. Several reviews are summarized with bibliographic information about the sources from which they were drawn. A subject and title index are located in the back.

Book review index. (1965-). Detroit: Gale Research, Annual.

> This periodical index provides references to reviews found in several dozen magazines and journals. It provides more citations than the *Book review digest* but does not provide excerpts from each review.

Dictionaries

The primary function of a dictionary is to define words. They often also provide pronunciation and guides to usage of words. Dictionaries can be *unabridged* or *abridged*, depending on the scope of the work. An unabridged dictionary attempts to include *all* words in a language and a comprehensive guide to usage. As you might guess, unabridged dictionaries are quite large. In fact, unabridged dictionaries are such massive undertakings to develop that there aren't very many available. An abridged dictionary is a smaller desk dictionary designed for everyday use. Dictionaries can also be *descriptive* or *prescriptive*. A descriptive dictionary merely records modern language and does not attempt to determine correct usage. A prescriptive dictionary can be considered a guardian of language since it recognizes that usage standards exist.

There are general dictionaries, specialized dictionaries, foreign language dictionaries, and subject dictionaries. Subject dictionaries exist for all sorts of subjects and define specialized terms in their field. They are listed in the last three chapters of this book.

Webster's new international dictionary of the English language, unabridged (2nd ed.). (1934). Springfield, MA: Merriam.

> Although this dictionary is older, libraries often keep it in their collection because it is unique. It advocates how words should be used. It is the classic unabridged prescriptive dictionary.

Webster's third new international dictionary of the English language, unabridged. (1961). Springfield, MA: Merriam.

This edition is quite different from the 1934 edition. It added modern words and dropped obsolete ones. Controversial at the time of its printing, it included words considered slang or inappropriate for such a record of the English language.

The American heritage dictionary of the English language. (3rd. ed.). (1992). Boston: Houghton Mifflin.

This dictionary focuses on the English language as it is used in the United States. This desk dictionary is designed for everyday use for the college student.

Acronyms, initialisms and abbreviations dictionary (Vols. 1-3). (1960-). Detroit: Gale Research.

What does NASA stand for? How about TOESL? Traditional dictionaries usually overlook such acronyms and abbreviations. This annual directory attempts to list such terms found in all fields, including science, technology, and education.

Roget's 21st century thesaurus in dictionary form. (1992). New York: Dell.

At times it is necessary to substitute one word for another that is alike in meaning. Some standard dictionaries provide this service up to a point. But in order to find synonyms and antonyms, plus definitions and uses of both, use a dictionary designed for that purpose. Roget's thesauri have been used by college students and writers for decades.

A dictionary of slang and unconventional English (8th ed.). (1984). New York Macmillan.

Most dictionaries deal principally with conventional language. They often ignore slang and jargon. This dictionary includes these ignored words, providing definitions and quotations. They can be useful in defining unfamiliar words in literature and song lyrics.

Dictionary of foreign phrases and abbreviations (2nd ed.). (1972). New York: H. W. Wilson.

A foreign language dictionary translates foreign words into English and vice versa. This dictionary translates phrases and abbreviations in several languages.

Below are listed a number of common foreign language dictionaries for a specific language. More can be found on the online catalog by conducting a keyword search for the name of language and the word "dictionaries," such as *Portuguese and dictionaries*, or by conducting a subject search, such as: *Portuguese language--dictionaries*.

Vox new college Spanish and English dictionary: English-Spanish/Spanish-English. (1984). Lincolnwood, IL: National Textbook.

Collins German-English, English-German dictionary: Unabridged (2nd ed.). (1993). New York: Ernst Klett Verlag.

Collins Robert French-English English-French dictionary (2nd ed.). (1990). New York: Harpercollins.

Directories

Directories list information about organizations, businesses, institutions, and individuals. The information provided can range from brief, as found in a phone book, to such information as addresses, names of officers, number of members or employees, a list of publications or products, and other related information. Product catalogs and college catalogs are directories. They can be about specific types of organizations, such as *Thomas Register of American Manufacturers* and *International Directory of Biomedical Engineers*, or general in nature, such as those in the following list.

> Note: The title of any book is determined by the authors, editors and publishers of that work. Directories often have words such as "encyclopedia" or "handbook" in their title. This does not stop them from *being* directories. The best way to evaluate a resource is to examine its contents yourself.

Encyclopedia of associations. (1956-). Detroit: Gale Research Company, Annual.

> This three-volume directory provides information about over 30,000 trade, business, social, and recreational organizations in the U.S. and Canada. It is organized by broad subject categories, but is best accessed by the index in the last volume. It provides contact information for the organization, along with publications or other activities. A separate set provides information on international organizations, *Encyclopedia of Associations: International Organizations.*

Internships. (1981-). Princeton, NJ: Peterson's Guides.

> This guide is from the same company that publishes Peterson's guide to four year colleges. This is a directory of companies that regularly offer internships in twenty-seven career areas. The directory provides a description of the company, the internships available, pay, benefits, and how to apply.

National directory of state agencies. (1974/75-). Gaithersburg, MD: Cambridge Information Group Directories.

> Every state has departments to handle such functions as issuing drivers licenses, protecting child welfare, collecting taxes, and issuing business licenses. This directory lists the addresses and phone numbers for such offices for all states plus the U.S. possessions (Puerto Rico, Guam, etc.).

Other examples of directories:

Bed and breakfast U. S. A.

Guide to 150 popular college majors.

Madison avenue handbook.

Peterson's hidden job market 1997: 2,000 fast-growing high-technology companies that are hiring now.

Sports fan's connection.

Summer jobs for students.

Internet Resources

AT&T 800 Directory on the Internet. [Online]. Available http:// www.tollfree.att.net/dir800/

CASE IN POINT

A student needs to give a ten minute speech on a topic of her choosing. She would like to do something about bicycling but isn't sure where to find information in the library. A general encyclopedia and a sports encyclopedia could be consulted for an overview and history of the sport. She could then narrow her topic, say to Tour de France. For further research, an almanac may provide a list of recent winners. Periodical indexes may lead her to articles in such magazines as *Sports Illustrated*.

Encyclopedias

Encyclopedias are excellent resources for exploring research topics and getting an overview of a topic. They are often the second place (after an almanac) a librarian goes to find information. While almanacs and dictionaries provide brief pieces of information, an encyclopedia goes in depth with long written articles. Many encyclopedias provide a short bibliography of books or journal articles at the end of each article. Some encyclopedias have yearbooks, such as the *World Book Year Book* and the *Britannica Book of the Year*. Their purpose is to keep the encyclopedia up-to-date.

General purpose encyclopedias cover the widest variety of subjects, while special encyclopedias can be very narrow in scope. Specialized encyclopedias exist for many subject areas. They are covered in the second section of this book.

The new encyclopaedia Britannica (Vols 1-32). (15th ed.). (1990). Chicago: Encyclopaedia Britannica.

Probably the most famous of all English language encyclopedias, it was originally published in England and is now published in the U.S. With this encyclopedia, the two volume index should be used first. The user will be directed to articles in the brief Micropaedia and/or the longer Macropaedia section.

Encyclopedia Americana (Vols 1-30). (1990). Danbury, CT: Grolier.

This is the oldest encyclopedia published in America. Its scholarly level makes it a good choice for college students. Its articles are arranged in a traditional A-Z format.

Collier's encyclopedia (Vols 1-24). (1949-). New York: Collier.

Collier's rounds out the list of three most popular adult encyclopedias. Collier's is directed toward upper high-school, lower college level students. Lists of resources for further reading are all grouped in the last index volume.

World book encyclopedia (Vols 1-22). (1995 ed.). (1995). Chicago: World Book.

This set is the most popular with students in upper elementary grades through high school. It can be useful to college students because it explains a subject briefly but thoroughly and has more illustrations than other sets.

Gazetteers

A gazetteer is a geographical place-name directory. It lists villages, cities, rivers, mountains, lakes, and other geographical places and features. A dictionary-type gazetteer may include information on a place's history, economy, and physical features such as latitude, longitude, and altitude. Often an atlas will contain a gazetteer that only provides locational information such as latitude and longitude.

Columbia Lippincott gazetteer of the world. (1962). New York: Columbia University Press.

> This work is very comprehensive, with over 130,000 entries. It has great historical value, but because of its age, another resource should be consulted for current information.

Webster's new geographical dictionary. (1988). Springfield, MA: Merriam.

> This gazetteer has less than 50,000 entries, but is the new standard in college libraries.

Internet Resources

> **U.S. Department of Commerce, Bureau of the Census.** *U.S. Gazetteer.*
> **[Online]. Available: http://tiger.census.gov/cgi-bin/gazetteer**

Handbooks and Manuals

Handbooks and manuals are quick-reference tools. A handbook contains a multitude of facts on a topic, such as a handbook of chemistry. Another type of handbook is *The Guinness Book of World Records*. A manual is a "how to" or "what is" book that deals with a specific subject area, whether it is preparing desserts or working on a motorcycle. One common type of manual is a style manual for writing papers.

> Note: As you will see, handbooks and manuals don't necessarily have the word "handbook" or "manual" in their titles. In fact, other words like "guide" or "encyclopedia" could be in their title instead. This does not stop them from *being* handbooks and manuals. The best way to evaluate a reference work is to examine it yourself.

Guinness book of world records. (1956-1990). New York: Sterling. (1991-). New York: Facts on File.

> This famous work lists holders of hundreds of world records and is heavily illustrated.

Hamachek, A. *(1995). Coping with college: A guide for academic success.* Boston: Allyn and Bacon.

> This guide helps students orient themselves to the college environment. It helps with motivation and study skills.

Kane, J. (1981). *Famous first facts* (4th ed.). New York: Facts on File.

> While this book may seem to contain pointless trivia, librarians find themselves using it over and over again to help students with assignments and research papers. It lists the first person to do just about anything, such as the first woman in Congress, or the first atomic bomb explosion. The book has an American slant. For instance, the entries on divorce and beer lists the first in America, although these events definitely happened earlier outside America.

Turabian, K. (1996). *A manual for writers of term papers, theses and dissertations* (6th ed.). Chicago: University of Chicago Press.

> This manual is the sourcebook for the "Turabian" bibliographic style.

U.S. Bureau of Labor Statistics. (1949-). *Occupational outlook handbook*. Washington, DC: U.S. Government Printing Office.

> This extremely useful resource provides information about occupations, including nature of the work, working conditions, training requirements, job outlook, earnings, and related occupations. The information is updated every two years.

All sorts of handbooks exist on various topics. They can be found using the online catalog. Some include:

Building a mail order business: A complete manual for success.

Chilton small engine repair.

Federal firearms regulations reference guide.

How to fix almost everything.

Inventing and patenting sourcebook.

The vegetarian traveller.

Quotation Books

Along with a dictionary and a thesaurus, the quotation book is an indispensable tool for a writer. Quotations add character to a paper, essay, or speech. There are a large number of quotation books available. Since they are all vary in scope and content, libraries carry quite a variety of them. If you don't find an appropriate quote in one book, try another. Your subject area may also have a specialized quotation book.

Bartlett, J. (1980). *Familiar quotations* (15th ed.). Boston: Little, Brown and Company.

> Also known as *Bartlett's Familiar Quotations*, this work is the classic of the field. It is arranged by author (person who originally made the quote). Unless the author is already known, it is best accessed by the extensive keyword index in the back.

Brussell, E. E., (Ed.) (1988). *Webster's new world dictionary of quotable definitions* (2nd ed.). New York: Webster's New World.

> Arranged in alphabetical order, it concentrates on quotations that somehow define a word or concept.

Respectfully quoted: A dictionary of quotations requested from the Congressional Research Service. (1987). Washington, DC: Library of Congress.

> Librarians conducting research for members of Congress compiled and published this book. It is based on requests received in the Library of Congress over the years. It is a very good resource for otherwise hard-to-find quotes.

BENJAMIN FRANKLIN

Finding Reference Resources

There are a number of ways to locate appropriate reference resources: searching the online catalog, consulting a book of reference resources, asking a reference librarian, and browsing the reference shelves. The library online catalog can be searched by author, title, or topic. Some online systems allow the user to search just the reference collection. If the topic is not found in the catalog, it may be because it is too specific or that the topic is not used as a subject in the catalog. For instance, if a search of German culture returns no library items, try searching for a broader topic such as "European Culture" or just "Culture."

Another strategy is to consult a guide to reference books. They will list reference resources under a variety of subjects. Two major guides are:

American reference books annual. (1970-). Englewood, CO: Libraries Unlimited.

> This annual publication lists reference works, with contributing authors providing reviews for each item. It contains a complete index.

Balay, R. (Ed.). (1902-). *Guide to reference books* (11th ed.). Chicago: American Library Association.

> This well known guide (to librarians at least) has been published since 1902. It lists over fourteen thousand resources, often providing the call number at which it can be found in the reference room. At the end is a complete author, title, and subject index.

A third way to locate reference materials is to consult with a reference librarian. They are highly trained in helping clients, and may be able to provide answers that will save a lot of time and frustration. The librarians also have written quite a number of help sheets, called "pathfinders." They provide lists of resources on commonly requested subjects.

A fourth, and definitely not the least helpful, method of finding reference materials, is to browse the reference shelves. One can run across all sorts of useful items not retrieved by other methods. You

---

CASE IN POINT

A student needs to write a position paper on Gulf War Syndrome. She needs to pick a position, either for or against the existence of this controversial condition. Figure 6.1 illustrates the kinds of information that could be found in the reference area . Faced with all these choices, the student should first think about what she needs. Since it is a controversial topic, she should look for people's firsthand accounts attesting to the existence of the condition. These could be found in newspapers and magazines such as *Time* and *Newsweek*. Since the federal government in the past has denied the existence of a "syndrome," she could read government reports to learn that side of the issue. She may also choose some other resources for more background information and statistics.

should not rely completely on this method, however, because many good resources may be available in other sections of the reference room. If a student were researching Gulf War Syndrome, for instance, and browsed in the military science section, he might overlook very useful items among the medical items, politics items, and general reference items.

Selecting and Evaluating Reference Resources

The library may have a number of reference resources on your topic. The task now is to decide which of the types of reference resources will be best for you. When faced with an information need in the library ask two questions:

1) What information do you need?
2) How much information do you need?

The first question is about the subject being researched. Answering this question can be difficult if you haven't chosen the subject of your research yet. If this is the case, you need to browse through materials until you select a topic. The second question refers to the depth of the information needed. Some people only require a few facts to answer a question. Other people need as much information as they can find. The different kinds of reference resources provide different kinds of information on a subject.

As you use reference resources, as with all information, examine the work. Is this information accurate? Is it up-to-date? Use the following six criteria to evaluate a work:

1. **Authority**. What or who is the source of this information? Was it written by a scholar, a government department, a private organization? Knowing the origin of the information can provide insight on how reputable the reference resource is.

2. **Purpose of Publication**. Was the information compiled to inform readers or to promote one side of a controversial subject?

3. **Accuracy**. This may be difficult to tell unless any errors are very obvious. Compare the information to another resource. Do they match? Check footnotes or other credits to determine a possible reason for any discrepancies. Since many statistical resources overlap in content, it is often easy to find a "second opinion."

4. **Currency**. How recent is the information? Think about the subject you are researching. Have there been any major developments since the information was published? Consider that it takes about a year for a manuscript to be published. The information is probably at least several months older than the copyright date. In some fields, particularly law and technology, those months and years can be critical.

5. **Scope**. How in-depth is the information treated? If a resource only provides basic information when you require lots of detail, you need to seek out additional resources.

Figure 6.1

Reference Resource Options

Topic: Gulf War Syndrome

Needed information	Appropriate reference sources
Contemporary accounts in newspapers and magazines	Periodical and newspaper Indexes
Books	Online catalog

Government Documents, such as:
      Department of Defense reports
      Congressional debates
      Presidential speeches
      EPA reports
	Online catalog and Government Documents index

Overview of Persian Gulf War history	Subject or general encyclopedia
Military Personnel statistics	Almanacs
Definition of technical terms	Dictionaries

(concept borrowed from Bolner Dantin & Murray, p. 147)

6. **Organization**. Is the resource easy to use? Are you forced to spend more time than necessary looking for pertinent information?

References

Bolner, M., Dantin, D, & Murray, R. (1991). *Library research skills handbook.* Dubuque, IA: Kendall-Hunt Publishing.

GOVERNMENT DOCUMENTS

We live in a country whose government is led by elected officials. The decisions of these government leaders are strongly influenced by our opinions which they hear directly via our letters, telephone calls, email, and our vote, and indirectly through the media. This system relies on our being well-informed about governmental activities, to read and listen to the news and sometimes to explore the official publications, the government documents, that report on those governmental activities. Robinson (1988), who teaches about documents, describes them:

> Government publications are generated as part of the daily business of government, to fulfill official duties and serve the public. While some government publications are written especially for the general public, most are issued to record actions or deliberations, to meet legal requirements, or to satisfy administrative needs. As deadly as this may sound, government documents are among the most valuable information sources in existence (p. 1).

Besides letting us know what our government is doing, government documents also supply a wealth of useful information. One of the best locations for finding this information is the government documents depository. The U.S. Government has established about 1400 federal documents depositories in libraries. Charged with the mission of making those publications available to the public, these depositories are found in all kinds of libraries across the country. Besides U.S. Government depositories, several state governments have established depositories for state publications. Check with your librarian to see if your library is a depository for state or federal documents.

Government publications have a reputation for being difficult to find and, once found, difficult to use. The goal of this chapter is to reduce the suffering associated with finding and using government publications by providing descriptions, instructions, and advice that will make using them much easier.

National, state, and local governments produce government publications. Local publications fall into three categories: those published by some private publisher (as notices in the local newspaper or the *Polk City Directory*), documents published by the city or some other public agency in the city, and those public records at the local courthouse. State publications commonly are published by state agencies at public expense. National publications are published by the federal government at public expense, although there are notable exceptions. International publications include those published by the United Nations and publications of foreign governments. Many international documents collections also include publications of universities in other countries.

Libraries make government documents available to the public. Libraries organize, house, and make accessible those documents which they accept from the federal or state government. A library may choose to be a regional or selective depository. A regional depository accepts all available documents, while a selective depository accepts, by prearrangement, those titles for certain subject areas and those that are mandatory for all depositories.

Local Documents

The lowest level of government is local government: county, city, village - any governmental unit below the state level. Local government information is often the most difficult to find because local governments seldom publish information themselves. Information such as proceedings of city council meetings and other city business is usually published in the local newspaper. Additional information may be available at various city offices. Below is a typical list of publications that contain local information:

Code of Ordinances of the City of Warrensburg, Missouri. (1985-). Tallahassee, FL: Municipal Code.

Warrensburg City Plan. (1975). Warrensburg, MO: Show-Me Regional Planning Commission.

Daily Star Journal. (1865-). Warrensburg, MO: Star-Journal Publishing. (local newspaper)

Polk City Directory. Warrensburg, Missouri. (1996). Detroit, MI: R.L. Polk. (telephone directory)

State Documents

State documents are published by state government agencies for many of the same reasons documents are published by federal agencies: to report on activities and missions and to meet the demands of the law. Access to state documents, however, is not as certain as that for federal documents. Some states have instituted depository programs, some have not. Such a program ensures that publications are available to users and are preserved as an historic record of state government activities. Check the online catalog in your library or ask a librarian to discover whether your library has a state documents collection.

Internet Resources

[Missouri] State Government Homepage [Online]. Available: http://www.state.mo.us/

NASIRE sites of interest [Online]. Available: http://www.nasire.org/sites.html
This site contains links to the many states that provide state documents online.

PIPER Resources [Online]. Available: http://www.piperinfo.com/states/states.html

> ### THINK ABOUT THIS....
>
> A library that has a government documents section as a part of its collection actually has a library within the library. The government documents area of any library could probably stand alone as a separate library. It has its own classification system, reference sources, journals, maps, pamphlets, paper and electronic indexes, and even its own "personal" librarian. So when you are in the government documents area of your library remember that it is a library within a library.

In states with no depository system, learning about and locating documents can be difficult. If your library does not have a documents collection, you will want to work with a librarian to explore alternative strategies. These may include searching the online catalog of a large library in your state such as the State Library, or calling the agency directly and asking for the information.

In spite of the difficulties associated with finding state documents, they are a valuable resource. Among other materials, state publications include statistical information about education, social services, demographics, and safety. They also include descriptive information about services available from the state; a record of state legislative action, laws, and regulations; tourist and recreational information; economic development programs; natural resources; and much more. Below are examples of important state government publications.

Laws

Revised statutes of the State of Missouri. (1835-). Jefferson City, MO: Missouri General Assembly, Committee on Legislative Research.

Case Law

West's Missouri digest (2nd ed.). (1983-). St. Paul, MN: West Publishing.

South Western reporter. (1887-). St. Paul, MN: West Publishing.

Miscellaneous

Constitution: State of Missouri. (1995). Jefferson City, MO: Rebecca McDowell Cook, Secretary of State.

Missouri Historical Review. (1906-). Columbia, MO: State Historical Society of Missouri.

Official manual: State of Missouri. (1972-). Jefferson City, MO: Secretary of State.

Profiles of Missouri Public Schools. (1980-). Jefferson City, MO: Missouri Dept. of Elementary and Secondary Education.

Federal Government Documents

The federal government publishes more information than any other single publisher in the world. In 1995 the Government Printing Office distributed 20 million publications (63,000 titles) in paper, microfiche, and electronic formats to depository libraries alone (*Administrative Notes, 1996*). These publications originated from all three branches of the government, including all the executive departments and agencies, the federal court system, and Congress.

Early federal publications were printed by private firms until the Government Printing Office opened in March, 1861. Some agencies continued to let private firms print government publications until the Printing Act of 1895 became law, bringing more centralization to government printing. Today, Title 44 of the *United States Code* regulates government printing and binding.

There are three basic things a library has to agree to do to receive federal documents. First, they must agree to keep the materials a certain length of time. Second, they need to designate someone as the "documents" librarian. Finally, they must allow the general public to have access to the documents. Most of the 1,400 depository libraries in the country are "selectives;" they choose the groups of federal publications they will receive based on their users' interests. A much smaller group of depositories are designated as Regionals. They receive everything made available through the depository system and are charged with providing permanent access to U.S. government publications. Only 53 libraries are designated as regional depositories.

U.S. government documents are generally organized by agency, then by offices within agencies, and then by document series. The call numbers for U.S. Government documents are called SuDoc numbers (short for Superintendent of Documents, the person in Washington who is responsible for managing the entire depository system). Below is an example of a SuDoc number:

> TD   Agency -- Transportation
> 4.2:   Sub-agency -- FAA
> F 64/8 This particular document

Note that the period (.) in the SuDoc number is *not* a decimal point. Numbers following the period are whole numbers. Therefore, HE 20.30: will come on the shelf *before* HE 20.2001:.

The variety of call numbers used in the SuDoc system causes confusion. A couple of rules will simplify finding documents:

1. Nothing Before Something:

> A 89.2: B 14/2   **comes *before***
> A 89.2: B 14/2/participant

2. "Author number" before year: There are a number of pieces of information that can make up the end of a SuDoc number. They have a hierarchy and are arranged in that order. Although you don't need this second rule often, it comes in handy.

A	Author number	A 89.2: B14	**comes *before***
D	Date	A 89.2: 1994	**comes *before***
L	Letter	A 89.2: A	**comes *before***
N	Number	A 89.2: 65	**comes *before***
W	Word	A 89.2: hospitals	

Strategies for Finding Federal Documents

The online catalog may contain some or all government documents owned by your library. Listed below are other indexes and reference aids that help the library user to locate materials in federal documents collections. The government documents area has its own reference sources, i.e. almanacs, handbooks, manuals, journal indexes, etc. If you have problems using these strategies or with finding documents, ask for assistance.

CAT/PAC plus. (1976-present). [CD-ROM]. San Antonio, TX: Marcive.

> Use this for finding records for all government documents distributed through the depository program since 1976. Searches can generally be performed by author, title, subject, keyword, etc. in CD-ROM databases. Boolean operators can be used for combined searching.

Figure 7.1 is a example of a typical government document record in *CAT/PAC Plus*.

Monthly catalog of United States government publications. (1895-). Washington, DC: U.S. Government Printing Office.

> Referred to simply as the *Monthly Catalog* (or MoCat), it first appeared in 1895. It is cumulated semiannually and annually. Arranged by agency, the entries are accessed through several indexes, including author, title, Library of Congress subject, series/report number, and stock number. Unless you are sure of the author, title, series/report number, or stock number, you will normally use the subject index to find needed materials. In 1996 this title migrated from paper to CD-ROM and Internet access.

Figure 7.2 is a sample *Monthly Catalog* entry along with the various "fields" one would see in a main entry in the *Monthly Catalog*.

Official Congressional directory. (1888-). Washington, DC: U.S. Government Printing Office.

> For each Senator and Representative this directory gives information about their lives, their home and business addresses, members of their staff, and their term(s) of office. It also lists each House's committees, joint committees and subcommittees; election statistics; information on the Executive Branch (including departments and agencies); the Judicial Branch of the government; members of the U.S. Diplomatic Corps, plus the foreign diplomats and consular offices.

Figure 7.1

```
FORMAT:            book
CONTROL NBR:       23083855
LC CARD NBR:       72340823
SYSTEM NBR:        58548904
SYSTEM NBR:        (OCoLC)5785478
TITLE: A Directory of all good things that count to you
and me / compiled by the Selected Committee of What
Counts, House of Representatives, Ninety-seventh Con-
gress, first session.
EDITION:           Rev. ed.
PUBLISHER:         U.S. G.P.O.
DATE:              1980.
DESCRIPTION:       v, ill, 134 p. : 26 cm.
NOTES:             At head of title: Committee print.
```

Figure 7.2

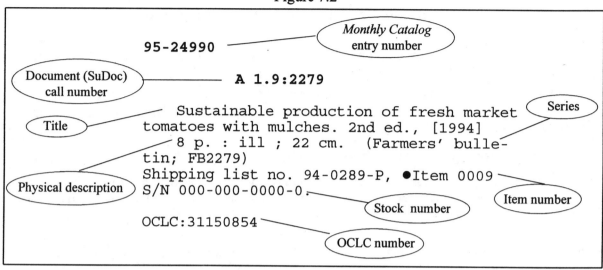

Occupational outlook handbook. (1949-). Washington, DC: U. S. Department of Labor.

> This vocational guidance source is used to help people choose and prepare for a career. It covers a wide variety of jobs, such as office occupations, education, health, science and technical fields, construction, transportation, social work, agriculture, etc. Each entry describes the nature of the work, training and qualifications, working conditions, advancement, earnings, future outlook, related occupations, and sources of additional information. The book has an index in the back.

National five-digit zip code and post office directory. (1981-). Washington, DC: U.S. Postal Service.

> All places, towns, and cities that have a post office appear in this annual directory. Each state is broken down by its smaller towns, which are assigned zip codes. Larger urban areas that require more than one zip code occupy the book's main portion. It is organized alphabetically by state then city name. All street addresses are given for these larger urban cities, and zip codes for these street names are listed.

Subject bibliographies. (1975-). Washington, DC: US Government Printing Office.

> Consult these for Hot Topics. They are annotated lists of recent documents organized by subject. Entries include stock number and price, as well as SuDoc number. They are updated on an irregular basis.

Statistical Information

Statistical abstract of the United States. (1879-). Washington, DC: U.S. Department of Commerce.

> Source for current popular information. Published every year, this is the basic reference guide both to major surveys conducted by the federal government and to information about regions, states, and private companies. Economic, political, and social statistics are the broad subject fields covered, with almost every topic imaginable accounted for within these subject fields. Begin searching by using the index located in the back. The index refers to table numbers, not page numbers.

American statistics index (ASI). (1973-). Washington, DC: Congressional Information Service.

> *ASI* was created to give access to government statistical information in government publications. If any federal publication contains statistics, it is covered by *ASI*. *ASI* has an index and an abstract section. Begin searching by topic in the Index volume; entry numbers will lead to descriptions in the Abstract volume.

Historical statistics of the United States, colonial times to 1970. (1975). Washington, DC: U.S. Bureau of the Census.

> Published by the U.S. Bureau of the Census, this supplement to the *Statistical Abstract* covers statistics to 1970. It contains statistics for about 8,000 different series, including the subjects of population, agriculture, energy, transportation, manufacturing and construction, prices, labor, and many more. An index is bound in the back.

County and city data book. (1949-). Washington, DC: U.S. Department of Commerce, Bureau of the Census.

> This work provides comprehensive statistical data for counties, cities, metropolitan areas, and those unincorporated places with a population of 2,500 or more. The data is primarily social and economic. Besides a wide coverage of subjects, this book provides explanatory notes, source citations, appendices, and geographical maps.

State and metropolitan area data book. (1979-). Washington, DC: U.S. Department of Commerce, Bureau of the Census.

> This reference tool presents a variety of statistical information for states and metropolitan areas in the U.S. The statistics are taken from the latest available census and deal with housing, manufacturers, local government, retail and wholesale trade, and other services. It also gives information on governmental and private agencies. Contents are listed in the front, and subject indexes to the tables are in the back.

United States government manual. (1935-). Washington, DC: U.S. Government Printing Office.

> The official handbook of the U.S. Government contains material on the programs and activities of both official and quasi-official agencies in its executive, judicial and legislative branches. Information is also given on international organizations, boards, committees, and commissions in which the U.S. has a part. Addresses and telephone numbers are also provided. A table of contents is found in the front, an index in the back.

Census Information

The U.S. Constitution calls for the federal government to count the population every ten years. Consequently, since 1790 census information has been collected and used to determine how many representatives a particular state sends to Congress. From the data collected, the U.S. Census Bureau creates several series of publications describing the residents of the nation by age, race, sex, type of housing, occupation, education, and much more. They also have an ongoing program for projecting population estimates between censuses which are used by schools, governments, and businesses to plan for the future and evaluate past performance.

CASE IN POINT

A student is looking for information about the use of drugs by college football players. She has found books and journal articles about the subject, but would like some personal experiences from people who have been associated with this problem. She is told to check in the Government Documents Area of the library. Why? Because government documents deal with all aspects of American life from family concerns and needs, sports, organized crime, science, health, education, art, the elderly, music, literature, etc. "Real" people often provide testimony of their experiences in congressional hearings. Various governmental reports cover a surprising range of topics. Chances are she will find sources to use for her paper.

1990 census of population general population characteristics. (1992). Washington, DC: U.S. Bureau of the Census.

> This series has a volume for each state. Each volume includes tables that describe the population in 1990 by their race, age and sex, household and family characteristics.

1990 census of population and housing summary population and housing characteristics. (1991). Washington, DC: U.S. Bureau of the Census.

> This series includes tables describing the population of each state by age, sex, race, household, and population density. It also gives greater detail about the type of housing, whether group quarters, apartments, rented or owned, and so forth.

Census data is also available on CD-ROM. Many disks use "GO" software, a simple menu-driven format that makes the most popular data easy to retrieve. Other disks include LANDVIEW software, a simple geographic information system, which presents the data linked to maps.

Earlier census information is summarized in *Historical Statistics of the United States, Colonial Times to 1970* and in the decennial census publications in the Government Documents collection.

Legislative Information

For the current Congress, the most recent information is available on the Internet at a site called GPO Access (see Internet Resources at the end of the chapter). Resources include the *Congressional Record*, congressional hearings, congressional bills and reports, laws, the *Congressional Directory*, House and Senate calendars, and much more. These electronic resources are searchable by keyword.

Senate and House bills and resolutions are also available in the library on microfiche. To find these, use the *Cumulative Finding Aid*. The *Cumulative Finding Aid* is an informal list updated weekly that advises which piece of microfiche to use to read a particular bill or resolution.

Other sources for legislative information include the *CIS Annual* for historical information and the *Monthly Catalog*, the annual listing of federal government publications.

Periodical Information

The federal government publishes hundreds of periodicals, most of which are not indexed in standard periodical indexes. Below are a couple of resources to access the articles in these periodicals.

U.S. government periodicals index (USGPI) [CD-ROM]. (1995-Present). Congressional Information Services.

> This does for government periodicals what the *Readers' Guide* does for commercial magazines, as both cover all manner of subjects. *USGPI* indexes about 180 government periodicals. Boolean operators aid in combining search words/phrases. This index provides the SuDoc and all the necessary information to form a bibliographic citation.

Figure 7.3 is a sample screen of what might expect to locate in one of the records.

NCJRS Document Database. (1991-). Washington, DC: U.S. Department of Justice.

This CD-ROM database indexes journal articles and research reports in criminal justice (See Chapter 12).

Other Document Formats

Government documents come in many formats besides paper books and pamphlets. They include maps, microfiche, CD-ROM, and Internet documents among others. Sometimes such alternative formats are necessary to best present the information at hand. For example, using large flat sheets of paper to display maps yields clear, easily-understood information to most users. Paper maps can be rolled or folded and carried into the field where they serve as useful and convenient guides to users. Other decisions, unfortunately, are not driven by the needs of users or the character of the information but are driven by congressional demands to save tax-payers' dollars and save space. Placing map information on microfiche meets the letter of the law (that agencies provide access, disseminate publications to depositories, etc.), but can make the information very difficult to use. A microfiched map may be easier to carry in a backpack, but the microfiche reader and the electric generator required to power it get heavy quickly. Whenever possible, depository librarians try to provide the most useful format possible.

Maps

First published by the federal government in the 1800s, maps are graphic, detailed representation of the usually earth's surface, although there are maps of the skies and underground maps. Topographic maps, such as those from the Geological Survey (USGS), Defense Mapping Agency (DMA) and the CIA are generally kept in large flat map drawers.

Microfiche

Microfiche is a form of micro printing on a 4" x 6" piece of film. Between 98 and 300 regular

Figure 7.3

```
ARTICLE TITLE:      What really counts when you need it.

AUTHOR:             Blow, Joseph

PERIODICAL:         Flying Right
ISSUING AGENCY: Air Force Safety Agency
DATE:           Feb 94 (9402)
VOLUME/NUMBER:      v22 , n1
PERIODICAL SUDOC:   D302.56:
DESCRIPTORS:        Humor ; Safety ; Conscience
USGPI ISSUE:        94-3
PERIODICAL NUMBER:  379
ACCESSION NUMBER:   94-23477-1
```

pages can fit on a single piece of microfiche, depending on how "micro" it is. The U.S. Government Printing Office began distributing documents printed on microfiche in the 1970s. This format was introduced to cut costs and save space.

CD-ROM

In the 1980s documents began arriving on CD-ROM. Advantages of the CD-ROM format include saving space and great portability--data can generally be copied to disk from most CDs into a text format and incorporated into word processing packages. The disadvantage is that one must have access to a computer and software that runs compact disks in order to view the document.

Internet

In the early 1990s a few government agencies began experimenting with placing government documents on the World Wide Web. Many federal court decisions, congressional bills, and an assortment of other documents are available on the Internet. An advantage of Internet distribution is that documents can be accessed at any Web-capable computer in the world. People don't have to go to one of the 1,400 depository libraries to read the documents. A drawback is that all depository libraries are not yet equipped with computers and Internet connections. Another drawback is that some forms of information, such as maps and other large documents, don't fit well on a computer screen.

International Documents

International documents include those published by the United Nations and other international organizations. The United Nations does have a depository program, however a much smaller number of libraries participate in it than the federal depository program. Most libraries purchase a selection of UN documents as they would regular books and other publications.

International documents also include those published by foreign government agencies. Some libraries build their collections with the help of exchange agreements with foreign governments. Others just purchase them singly. Some international information is also available on the Internet. An example is the homepage for the Foreign Ministry of Japan at *http://nttls.co.jp/infomofa*. A good place to begin searching for foreign sites on the Internet is at a web subject index such as Yahoo. See the next chapter for details.

Conclusion

Documents collections are the place to find out what state and national governments are doing. They are also a great place for finding primary materials like census statistics and the record of congressional and executive office activities. Because of their nature, documents sometimes require using different search strategies. They also have call numbers that work in a slightly different manner than Library of Congress or Dewey call numbers. Using the strategies and tips above and asking for assistance will make the documents collections easier to use.

> ## Case in Point
>
> You are preparing a report on the education of populations in certain counties. More specifically, you are wanting to compare the educational attainment of populations where regional universities are located against the county populations where no college or university resides. In order to support your thesis that populations in counties where there is a state university has a higher percentage of college graduates, you will need some statistical data. This is the type of information you would find in census reports.

Reference

Robinson, J. S. (1988). *Tapping the government grapevine: The user-friendly guide to U.S. government information sources.* Phoenix, AZ: Oryx.

Internet Resources

General and Judicial Branch:

GPO Access. [Online]. Available: http://access. gpo. gov/su_docs/aces/aces002.
   html

Cornell University   [Online]. Available: http://www. law. cornell. edu/

University of Michigan. [Online]. Available: http://www. lib. umich. edu/libhome/
   Documents. center/index. html

Villanova University [Online]. Available: http://ming. law. vill. edu/

Legislative Branch:

THOMAS. [Online]. Available: http://thomas.loc. gov/

Senate. [Online]. Available: http://www. senate. gov/

House of Representatives. [Online]. Available: http://www. house. gov/

Executive Departments and Agencies:

Census Bureau. [Online]. Available: http://www. census. gov

Bureau of Justice. [Online]. Available: http://www. usdoj. gov/

Federal Aviation Administration. [Online]. Available: http://www. tc. faa. gov/

Whitehouse. [Online]. Available: http://www. whitehouse. gov/

International

AdmiFrance: L'annuaire des services internet de l'administration francaise/direc-
   tory of french government Internet services. [Online]. Available: *http://
   www.admifrance.gouv.fr/cgi-bin/multitel/admifrance/sommaire*

The Federal Commission for the Securities Market (Russia). [Online]. Available:
   http://www.fe.msk.ru/iso/infomarket/fedcom/ewelcome.html

Foreign Ministry of Japan. [Online]. Available: *http://www.mofa.go.jp/*

South African Constitutional Assembly. [Online]. Available: *http://
   www.constitution.org.za/*

THE INTERNET

What is the Internet? The Internet is a worldwide network made up of other computer networks. It interconnects the simplest personal computers and the most sophisticated supercomputers with a variety of telecommunication systems. We can only estimate exactly how big the Internet is because its size changes daily, even hourly. Currently there are probably several million computers on the Internet with approximately ten times that many users. All of these computers can communicate with one another through the same communication standards known as Transmission Control Protocol/Internet Program or TCP/IP.

Michael Gorman sums up the organizational structure of the Internet by stating:

> The net is like a huge vandalized library. Someone has destroyed the catalog and removed the front matter, indexes, etc., from hundreds of thousands of books and torn and scattered what remains . . . and the walls are covered in graffiti. "Surfing" is the process of sifting through this disorganized mess in the hope of coming across some useful fragments of text and images that can be related to other fragments. The net is even worse than a vandalized library because thousands of additional unorganized fragments are added daily by the myriad cranks, sages, and persons with time on their hands who launch their unfiltered messages into cyberspace (Gorman, 1995, p. 32-34).

This statement may seem somewhat humorous, but it is more close to the truth than one may like to admit. There is no single individual or organization that runs the Internet. The Internet is the collective effort of many thousands of individuals and organizations in many countries. The users of the Internet have access to thousands of discussion groups where users converse about different topics, library catalogs and databases on different subjects, software programs, computer and text files, images, music, video, courseware, and, of course, electronic mail. The major features of the Internet can be placed into five categories: Email, Telnet, File Transfer Protocol (FTP), Gopher, and the World Wide Web (WWW).

History of the Internet

What was to be known as the Internet (it wasn't actually termed the "Internet" until the early 1980s) began in the 1960s as a way to make sure communication lines would be available in case the United States was attacked by a foreign nation. Researchers, funded by the U.S. Department of Defense, began experimenting with linking computers to each other through normal telephone hook-ups. The project was titled "Advanced Research Projects Agency (ARPA)." Before this, all computers operated completely independently of each other. If one wanted to share information with people working on a different computer, the information had to be loaded onto reel-to-reel tapes and delivered physically to the other site.

ARPA wanted to see if computers in different locations could be linked using a new technology known as packet switching, which had the promise of letting several users share just one communications line. Previous computer networking efforts had required a direct line between each computer on the network that operated like a train track on which only one train could travel at a time. The packet system allowed for creation of an electronic highway with several lanes shared by a large numbers of vehicles. Each message was broken down into several small packets. Each packet was given the computer equivalent of a roadmap and a assembly number so that it could be sent to the right destination, and then reassembled into a message the computer or a human could use. Today the same technology is still in use.

In the beginning there were three components — email, telnet and ftp. All three of these still exist and can be used in conjunction with the WWW (World Wide Web). Ftp, or file transfer protocol, is used to send or retrieve computer files to or from other computers. Telnet is used to "log on" to a remote computer and use it as if working from a directly wired terminal. Email, or electronic mail, is used to send messages to the computer address of another user. Email was originally the least important component of the Internet.

In the 1970s, ARPA took on the role of developing rules, or protocols, for transferring data between different types of computer networks. These Internet (from "internetworking") protocols made it possible to evolve into the worldwide network we have today. By the close of the 1970s, links were constructed between ARPANet and its counterparts in other countries. The world was now tied together in a computer web. In 1983 the military part of the network, MilNet, split from ARPANet to carry only Department of Defense traffic.

In the 1980s, the Internet, expanded very quickly. Hundreds, then thousands, of colleges, research institutions, and government agencies began to connect their computers to the network. Now anybody with a computer and modem—and persistence—can take part.

The Internet, with its three components, ftp, telnet, and email, stayed largely the same until "gopher" was developed by the Computer and Information Services Department at the University of Minnesota and released for public use in 1991. Gopher, a kind of electronic bulletin board system, caught on a very quickly as it was an easy way to "post" information for general audiences. As a result, universities and other users began to create their own gopher sites to post information. Directories, research reports, university phonebooks, schedules of classes, all sorts of information became available in electronic format. A new way of publishing information was begun.

In January 1993 the Internet consisted of about 1.3 million computers. Today that number is estimated at well over 16 million (Network Wizards, 1997). Internet computers, called hosts or sites, store data available for retrieval. Thousands of public mailing lists, hundreds of libraries, and many thousand Usenet newsgroups are available, and these are just the big categories.

The latest big development in Internet-land was the World Wide Web (WWW) by CERN in

Switzerland in 1991 (the first web browser, Mosaic, wasn't available until 1993). The Web took the concept of providing public information, as gopher does, and advanced it. The hypertext organization, explained later in this chapter, meant that people no longer had to memorize strange commands and protocols for using ftp and gopher. World Wide Web software, called browsers, handle the specifics of Internet communication. Older Internet applications are text based, with information limited to typewriter-like characters on a blank background. The Web's graphical interface makes the Web appealing to use but also requires powerful computers and high speed Internet communications. The development of desirable applications have driven people and organizations to upgrade their computer systems to keep up.

A present development is in building substantive Internet sites that offer valuable and useful information. Another development is increasing web capabilities supporting sound, graphics, and moving graphics such as films and other memory intensive applications.

Email

Email, short for electronic mail, is by far the most popular application on the Internet today. It is an extremely powerful tool that is simple to use and easy to understand. Using email can give you a real feel for the energy and reach of the Internet. With email you can communicate just as easily with someone out-of-state as you can with someone in the same building. Your individual message can be sent to a single person, or it can reach hundreds of Internet users at the same time. Email is very fast. It is sent and received in seconds - minutes at most. Postal mail is often called "snail mail" by comparison. Electronic mail on the Internet is primarily text, but it is possible to send other formats such as graphic images as long as they are encoded to text before sending and converted back to original format upon receipt. This switching is automatically done by many computers on the Internet.

This system allowed computers to share electronic data and researchers to exchange email. In itself, email was something of a revolution, allowing users to send detailed letters at a fraction of the speed of a phone call. (In actuality, email was not foreseen as being important in the development of Internet. It was fun but not a serious application. Today the majority of Internet traffic is email.)

Sending email is not difficult. All you need is access to the Internet, an email program, and the email address of the person with whom you wish to communicate. Similarly, if someone wants to send you a piece of email they need your email address.

Figure 8.1

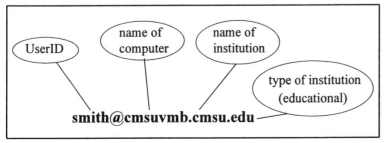

smith@cmsuvmb.cmsu.edu

An Email address, like a postal mail address, contains all the necessary information needed to deliver a message to someone. Each email address is different, although they all consist of two parts -- a local part and a host part. These two parts are separated by an "@" sign. Figure 8.1 shows an example of an email address.

An Email message has three basic parts, the header, body, and signature. The "header" contains the information about *who, what* and *where* — *who* sent the message, *what* the message is about, and *where* they reside in Internet-land (their email address). The "body" of the email message is the message itself. The final part of the message is the "signature" of the sender. The signature is at the end of the message and gives information about the sender, such as name, title, email address, phone number, mailing address, FAX number, etc.

Email programs usually have some kind of "reply" feature that makes it easier to respond quickly and easily to a message without have to initiate the answer on your own. The reply feature takes care of filling in the address and subject field (using information in the original message's header) and leaves only the typing of the response.

At this time there is no comprehensive online directory assistance for email addresses comparable to those for telephone numbers. There are ways to find email addresses, and the more proficient you become in using the Internet, the more tricks you will learn. *There is nothing wrong with just calling and asking for someone's email address.* A trend these days is to include your email address on your business card.

ListServs

ListServ discussion groups exist to allow users who have a common interest (biology, food, flying, cats, history, cars) to correspond with one another via email. There are thousands of Lists. By subscribing to a List, you will automatically receive email messages from the List. You can send a message to the List, and it in turn will be distributed to everyone who has a subscription. If you find out that the List is no longer of interest, you can Unsubscribe to it. It does not cost any money to belong to a ListServ.

ListServs were developed very shortly after email. As the "ARPANet" system evolved some enterprising college students developed a way to use it to conduct online conferences. These started as science-oriented discussions, but they soon branched out into virtually every other field, as people realized the power of being able to communicate with people around the country (The television series Star Trek was one of the major subjects).

Internet Resources

Bigfoot [Online]. Available http://bigfoot.com/

email directory for the online community. It us used to find the email addresses of others. You can also create your own listing.

Lizst directory of email discussion groups [Online]. Available: http:// www.liszt.com/

CASE IN POINT

You enjoy traveling. In fact, you enjoy traveling so much that you decide you would like to belong to a Listserv discussion group that shares travel experiences. You find a reference to just such a group called TRAVEL-L. It has two email addresses associated with it:

List Address (mail to): **TRAVEL-L@vm3090.ege.edu.tr**
Administrative Address (commands to): **listserv@vm3090.ege.edu.tr**

To subscribe to the TRAVEL-L List, send a message to **listserv@vm3090.ege.edu.tr**. In the body of the message, type *subscribe TRAVEL-L Firstname Lastname*. After receiving messages from it for several days, you decide to share with the group your opinion of the hotels in Cancun, Mexico. You send your message to **TRAVEL-L@vm3090.ege.edu.tr** and tell your story. Your message is sent to all the subscribers, some of whom will comment on your opinions. Follow-up comments may go on for several days.

There are various ways to discover ListServs on different subjects. References can be found in classes, books, or magazines. Their name often ends with "-L" such as Travel-L, a discussion group on travel experiences. Lists of Lists can be found on the World Wide Web.

Two important pieces of information concerning a ListServ are its two email addresses, "commands to" and "mail to". The "commands" address is for subscribing and unsubscribing to the list. The "mail to" address is for distributing messages to the other members of the list. Although directions may vary, often one subscribes to the list by sending an email message to the "Commands To:" address. In the body of the message type SUBSCRIBE nameoflist YourFirstName YourLastName. The name of the list will be everything before the @ sign in the "Mail To:" address) In order to send messages to the list, one sends an email message to the "Mail To:" address.

Telnet

Before telnet, users were unable to logon to remote computers. Telnet allows the user to logon to a remote computer and then use the local keyboard to use the remote computer. It is not possible to telnet to all computers. The remote computer must allow distant users to logon. The user also needs to have the address and a password to the remote site.

Today, the most common use of telnet is to access online library catalogs. Using telnet allows searching of materials in thousands of libraries around the world. However, remember that foreign library catalogs may not be in English!

It is always a good idea to read the initial information offered by the remote system, because it offers the way to properly terminate the connection to the system. Otherwise you might have to invoke PLOTKA -- Press Lots of Keys To Abort.

CASE IN POINT

You are at home and want to see if the library has books on one of the several subjects you have chosen to write a paper. You could get dressed and go to the library, but it is raining cats and dogs outside. You have a computer in your dorm room that allows you to use telnet and you have the address for the campus library, as well as the public library. You can telnet to the libraries' online catalogs to determine if enough material exists on your ideas. Sure, you still have to go to the library to get the material, but you have completed one major step in the research process -- choosing the subject.

File Transfer Protocol -- (ftp)

One of the most popular features of the Internet is the ability to get files from other computers. This feature alone was one of the main reasons that the Internet grew so quickly in its early years. Groups of researchers around the world could share data simply by putting it on one computer and then downloading it to their computers as needed. The basic program to transfer between computers is ftp.

Ftp has been around a long time, and its unfriendly interface shows it. Some ftp sites also support the gopher program, which is much friendlier and easier to use. Ftp is an important tool because sometimes that is the only way to access certain information.

The major difference between gopher and ftp is that in ftp one must know in advance the address of the computer with the desired information, and the location of the file on that computer. Many ftp files can now be accessed with gopher and the WWW making it unnecessary to keep exact records of sites and file names.

Internet Resources

Archie Servers:

AT&T server [New York] [Online]. Available: telnet://archie.internic.net

Rutgers University [New Jersey] [Online]. Available: telnet://archie.rutgers.edu

University of Nebraska [Online]. Available: telnet://archie.unl.edu

FTP sites:

CNET Inc. (1997). Download.com [Online]. Available: http:// www.download.com/

ZDNET Software Library [Online]. (1997). Available: http:// headlines.yahoo.com/zddownload/software/

Archie

The best way to sort through the millions of files available by anonymous ftp is with Archie, the gigantic database of files known to be publicly available. The Archie database doesn't know the contents of files, but if the name of the desired file is known and it is available, it can probably be found with Archie. After finding the names and locations of desired files, ftp is used to get the files themselves.

The Archie system is maintained by many universities and networking organizations. Most run the same software, and all share information on the best ways of making the database available to the widest audience.

It is now more common to search the World Wide Web for files available for download. Web browsing software will automatically initiate an ftp session for download.

Gopher

Gopher is an application that organizes access to Internet resources using a uniform interface that is simple to understand and easy to use. Basically, it is a client/server system (client software is the one loaded on your personal pc, server software is loaded on the host computer) that navigates through the Internet without using any confusing commands. The information is arranged in a hierarchical fashion; one moves through a series of menus to reach a desired destination. See an example of a gopher screen in Figure 8.2. When gopher as made available to the world in 1991, it represented a new way of storing and using information. In the past, one could download information from the Internet, but could only view or use the files later using another piece of software. For instance, a text document could be downloaded as a file, but could only be opened and read inside a word processor. Gopher allows the user to read and use the information at the time of connection. Gopher is strictly text based, however, pictures can be transferred as files, but they can not be viewed within the gopher. Gopher also masks many of the technical aspects of using the Internet. While it may not be evident to the user, Gopher involves doing things like transferring files, changing directories, telneting to computers, and querying servers all over the world.

The following is a list of some of the features of using Gopher:

*Directory trees are shown as lists. To choose a file to view or to transfer, it is not necessary to type its name.

*Entries are in plain text, not cryptic file names, and are thus easier to read.

*Links can be to files on other computers. This vastly reduces the amount of redundant information on the Internet. For instance, instead of copying some files from a host computer, gopher servers automatically access those files on their home server.

Internet Resources

> **[Veronica Server] [Online] Available: gopher://veronica.scs.unr.edu**
> **This server at the University of Nevada, Reno, lists all the known veronica database servers. It also has the latest guide to using veronica.**

*Gopher links to other services. For example, one can select an entry that automatically starts a telnet or ftp link to another computer.

*Most gopher clients can be customized. It is possible to store a bookmark to frequently accessed sites.

*Combined with Veronica, gopher servers can be searched for particular information.

With the development of the WWW, gopher sites are shrinking in number. Those that remain, however, are an efficient way to share information without using a lot of computer space.

Veronica

There are hundreds of Gopher servers on the Internet. In order to find one with particular information on a subject, gopher can be searched using a tool called "Veronica." The Veronica database indexes headings from virtually every Gopher server on the Internet and is reasonably easy to use.

Figure 8.2

```
Gopher Menu


    Read Me First
    Faculty and Staff Directory A-L
    Faculty and Staff Directory M-Z
    Campus Directory
    About Central Missouri State University
    State of Missouri and City of Warrensburg
    CMSU - Course Equivalencies
    Graduate Studies
    Central Fact Book
    College of Applied Sciences
    College of Business and Economics
    Department of Computer and Office Information System
    Department of Electronics Technology
    Department of Music
    Department of Physical Education
    Information Services
    Central Link
    Library Services
```

Central Missouri State University Gopher [Online] Available: gopher://
    cmsuvmb.cmsu.edu/

World Wide Web (WWW)

The World Wide Web is a graphical information storage and retrieval system. In contrast to Gopher's hierarchical organization, the World Wide Web offers documents, images, sound, and video in a *hypertext* style. A hypertext system allows documents to contain embedded "links" to other documents. Anyone creating a hypertext document can insert links to other documents of interest. This gives the reader the choice of moving from topic to topic at will. See Figure 8.3 for an example of a web page. The diagram in this book is unable to show the color, animations, and links that make a web page a living document. The goal of WWW is to make all online knowledge part of one web of interconnected documents and services.

What is hypertext? Hypertext is text connected to one or more other documents or items. As links are joined, they form a web. For instance, if one was reading a document about a baseball team, the document may provide links to related information such as individual players, recaps of recent games, or a picture of the stadium. Some sites are so interconnected that following links from one page to the next will bring you back to where you began. Once learned, though, it is very fast and flexible in the retrieval of information.

Each place, or resource, on the World Wide Web is called a "Web page." Each page has a unique address called a URL, or Universal Resource Locator. See Figure 8.4 for a description of the parts of a URL. Web pages can be developed by anyone with access to a Web server and the proper software. There are an estimated minimum of 16 million web servers in the world (Network Wizards, January 1997). In the early days of the Web most pages were created in universities. Presently, the fastest growing segment of the Web is the commercial sector. Many companies are finding the Web to be an ideal place to advertise their products.

The WWW has grown in popularity until it is now the second most popular Internet activity (following email). Because it can transmit large images, sound, and video files, users of the Internet have concerns about the Internet's ability to handle the rapidly growing traffic loads. Internet providers are responding by installing faster networks, but users find response times are considerable slower

THINK ABOUT THIS...

In the preceding text, it says that Web pages can be developed by anyone with access to a Web server and the proper software. What does this mean? In other media, such as television, radio, newspapers, and magazines, it costs a great deal of money to get space and/or airtime, and even more money to develop a catchy message. The cost of developing a Web site can be very low. Therefore, the Internet has become an attractive resource for small groups or individuals on small budgets. You can find information about all sorts of fringe political and social groups, people spreading gossip, anyone trying to grab attention. This can be a lot of fun, but the user needs to remember that information can be distorted or false. There is absolutely no way to force anyone to take out-of-date or untruthful information off the Internet. Therefore, surf with care.

Figure 8.3

Library Services

President's Welcome	Library Faculty
Discover Central	Library Staff
NY Times Bestsellers	Pat Antrim's **Govdocs**
Electronic journals	LIS Course Pages
Links/Search Page	Other Pages
Library Services Publications	New Books List

Telecommunications Advisory Group

Comments or Suggestions?

during peak-use hours.   This will continue until the major arteries of traffic, collectively called the "backbone," are increased in size, or "bandwidth." To reduce the number of problems with slow response, try using the WWW during evening and early morning hours.

There are three ways to move around and use resources on the World Wide Web. The first way is to browse the hypertext links. A number of web pages serve as indexes by categorizing Web resources by subject. One can go from link to link looking for desired information. Yahoo, described later, is a popular web index. The second way to "surf the 'Net" is to begin with a known address.

Figure 8.4

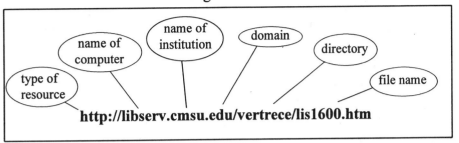

Type the address into a browser and go straight to the site. Addresses can be found in many places-in magazines, on television, in newspapers. A third way is to use a search engine. Very often a person wants to find information about a particular subject. A search engine will search portions of the Web and return a list of links. As with all electronic searching, one often has to experiment with the search words to receive an accurate list of links.

Web Browsers, Indexes, and Search Engines

The World Wide Web must be accessed with a personal computer. A number of different software programs, called browsers, are available. Once access is made to the Web, it can be searched, much like a magazine index, for useful information. The browsers, indexes and search tools listed below have many things in common. First, they are free. Second, they provide help screens which give information about the product and explanation of its use. Some of the systems are limited in capability, but the limitations do not prevent you from identifying and transferring valuable information (documents, pictures, graphics, sounds, etc.) to your computer. The best way to learn the value of each service is to connect to it and read the information offered.

Netscape 3.0 [Computer Software]. (1996). Mountain View, CA: Netscape Communications.

    Netscape is one of several client software programs that allows the user to navigate, or browse, the Web. It can be used in a Windows or Macintosh environment. It allows the user to work with most Internet applications — Web, telnet, gopher, or ftp. The user can connect to Web pages to navigate the links embedded within WWW documents.

Below are some of the more prominent navigation tools.

Yahoo [Online]. Available: http://www.yahoo.com

    Yahoo is one of the millions of pages on the Web. It serves as a subject index to Web sites. Yahoo categorizes Web sites by broad subject topics such as Arts, Business, Education, Government, Recreation, and Social Science. More specified sub-headings exist for the broader ones. For example, under "Social Science" there are sub-headings for Anthropology, Sociology, and Economics. Yahoo also contains a searching tool to search Web sites indexed within Yahoo. Boolean operators can be used to combine search terms.

URL ABBREVIATIONS

Types of Resources	Most Common Domains	
HTTP (HyperText Transfer Protocol)	com - commercial	ca - Canada
gopher	edu - educational	de - Germany
ftp	gov - government	jp - Japan
mailto (email)	net - Networks	uk - United Kingdom
	org - organization	us - United States

MetaCrawler [Online]. Available: http://metacrawler.cs.washington.edu:8080/index.html

MetaCrawler is another free search service that is a little different from others. As a matter of fact, it does not have its own internal database, but is reliant upon existing search engines such as Lycos, Webcrawler, etc. Searching in MetaCrawler takes the user to the other databases which in turn complete the search and forward the results back to MetaCrawler.

Search [Online]. Available: http://www.search.com

Search is another system, like Yahoo, that does a number of things. It is first an index, offering broad subject headings — Arts, Automotive, Employment, Legal, News, Science, and Travel, just to name a few. It also has links to other search engines.

The above sites are just a few of the navigation tools available on the Web. The search engines are by no means identical. They each index a different number of web pages and are constructed to search the web in different manners.

Summary

The information superhighway has become a reality. The Internet -- an interconnection of tens of thousands of public and private networks worldwide -- provides millions of users with access to information from around the globe. This complex network forms the initial pathway for the global information revolution that will eventually link businesses, public and private agencies, and educational centers with one another and with consumers in their homes.

Information is the substance of the Internet -- information that is exchanged through formal or informal communication among individuals or groups and information that is broadcast or made accessible to the general Internet community. This is also a drawback of the Internet because not all information is accurate or based upon research.

The challenge of using the Internet effectively is not in finding information. The challenge is in finding information that you are interested in while avoiding that which is not needed. Humans are well adapted to this sort of behavior, but most of us have not yet developed the skills in computer-mediated environments. When searching the Internet, even the most expert 'net surfers get frustrated when things are not where they are expected to be. Organization of material on the Internet is getting better and better, even though sites keep changing and moving. Many web sites are maintained by individuals on their own equipment, therefore they can delete or change material as they see fit.

The Internet is more than just a technological marvel. It is human communication at its most fundamental level. The pace may be a little quicker when the messages race around the world in a few seconds, but it's not much different from a large and interesting party. As it becomes easier to use, more and more people will join this worldwide community of several million. Before long being a citizen of cyberspace and having the world at your fingertips will seem like the most natural thing in the world, like picking up a phone or watching TV.

References

Dern, D. P. (1994). *The Internet guide for new users*. New York: McGraw-Hill.

Gorman, M. (1995, September 15). The Corruption of Cataloging, *Library Journal* 120, 32-34.)

Network Wizards (1997). *Internet domain survey, January 1997* [Online]. Available http://www.nw.com/zone/WWW/report.html

Newby, G. B. (1994). *Directory of directories on the Internet: A guide to information sources*. Westport: Meckler.

Tolhurst, W. A., Pike, M. A., & Blanton, K. A. (1994). *Using the Internet* (special ed.). Indianapolis: Que.

Internet Resources

Subject Indexes:

Magellan [Online]. Available: http://www.mckinley.com
> The index contains links to web sites that have been reviewed by the Magellan staff. It also includes a search engine for searching Magellan sites.

Infoseek Guide [Online]. Available: http://www2.infoseek.com
> This site bills itself as the "Web's largest directory." It categorizes web sites into 13 major categories, each with numerous sub-headings. It also offers a search engine.

The Argus clearinghouse [Online]. Available: *http://www.clearinghouse.net/*
> Students at the Library School at the University of Michigan put together this Web site to categorize web sites under subject headings.

WWW Virtual Library [Online]. Available: http://www.w3.org/vl/

Search Engines:

Alta Vista [Online]. Available: http://www.altavista.digital.com

DejaNews [Online]. Available: http://www.dejanews.com
> Only searches news group conversations - what most other search engines don't

Excite [Online]. Available: http://www.excite.com
> This search engine indexes several million web pages. It ranks search results by confidence.

SUBJECT SPECIFIC RESEARCH

The information and materials presented in the first eight chapters of this book have dealt with general subjects. The basic research skills learned up to this point will be very valuable for all kinds of college research. Regardless of topic, the steps for choosing library search tools and using them are still the same. The library materials presented so far have also been general in nature. The online catalog, as a rule, contains all materials owned by a library. General encyclopedias, dictionaries, and periodical indexes cover all topics to some extent. These resources do not claim to provide the most comprehensive information on any given subject; they are useful, however, and may be all that are required for certain quests for information.

You may be tempted to skip over the first part of this book and concentrate solely on specialized reference resources for your field. Many aspects of specialized fields, however, interact with general topics such as current events. Aviation safety, social issues, and natural disasters are all topics that intersect with public interest. A good information seeker will retain his or her ability to utilize the general information resources and may find that they often fill his or her needs.

In upper-level undergraduate and graduate courses the information needs in support of a research paper or project may require the use of more specialized resources. Much of this material may require previous knowledge or interest in the subject. As the student's knowledge of the subject content grows, he or she will learn to consult those information resources that will best suit the needs of the field.

Each subject discipline has characteristics that require unique information resources. In order to organize an overview of information resources into manageable components, this text uses three broad classifications for the information resources that support the knowledge base: the humanities, the sciences, and the social sciences.

The Humanities

The humanities include the disciplines which reflect the arts and culture of society. Subjects such as music, painting, sculpture, drama, motion pictures, languages, literature, poetry, history, anthropology, philosophy, and religion illustrate the broad scope of humanity in cultural achievements. The information resources for these areas are covered in Chapter 10.

Unlike the sciences, the majority of the humanities fields view the library as a learning laboratory. The performing and visual arts, including art, drama, and music, may have their studio laboratories, but the library is certainly a major contributor in support of any research activities of these fields. Another contrast between the humanities and other fields is the fact that currency of published materials is less likely to be a factor regarding the usefulness of the materials. In the humanities many classical works will have lasting relevance because the body of information in the field is less dynamic. One may add to that body of knowledge, but newer information is not so likely to render older published information obsolete as in the sciences and in the social sciences.

Throughout the 19th and the first half of the 20th centuries, the college degree earned by most college students was likely to be a bachelor's degree in the liberal arts. The proliferation of degrees in other subject areas is a fairly recent trend. Historically, the mark of a truly educated person was someone who was knowledgeable in a broad array of subjects: languages, literature, history, art, music, history, mathematics, science, geography, law, philosophy and political science. This type of education was what came to be the Bachelor of Arts degree in Liberal Arts. The bulk of the subject matter in a liberal arts degree is taken from areas of the humanities and still forms the basis of the general education that is a part of bachelor's degree programs in any college or university. One can see the importance of an understanding of the information resources that exist for these disciplines. Regardless of the degree one pursues, exposure to information in the humanities is still of value to the educated person.

The Sciences

Library materials for the sciences, both pure and applied, will be covered in Chapter 11. Applied science topics include (but are not limited to): agriculture, automotive technology, aviation, child development, construction, dietetics, electronics technology, fashion merchandising, graphics, home economics, hospitality management, industrial hygiene, industrial management, manufacturing, military science, nursing, power mechanics, safety science, and textiles and clothing. Pure science topics include biology, chemistry, computer science, earth science, geology, mathematics, physics, and zoology.

All the science & technology subjects listed above hold some characteristics in common when it comes to using the library:

1. Currency. When researching in these fields, students often find it necessary to look for as recent information as possible. Technology advances so rapidly that material becomes quickly dated. This is especially true where law and computer technology intersect with a topic.

The passage of important laws can completely change a field. In safety science, for instance, it would be foolish to rely on any works published before the Occupational Safety and Health Act (OSHA) passed in 1970 unless writing from a historical perspective. Similarly, it would be foolhardy to pilot a plane relying on a several years' old understanding of FAA regulations.

Computer technology, of course, is developing very quickly. Manufacturing, automotive technology, navigation, and graphics have changed tremendously. Advances in these fields make it a totally different world from even ten years ago. University faculty try to train students in the latest developments. Nothing, though, beats keeping up in one's field by reading journals.

2. Reliance on journal literature and research reports. As mentioned in Chapter 6, it takes a year or more for a manuscript to get published as a book. The editing process takes a lot of time. Serial publications, like journals, magazines, and newspapers are faster, although journals issued four times a year or less can still take up to a year to be published. Researchers submit their work to journals rather than books for timeliness. The one exception to this is when a professional organization holds a conference in which scholars and professionals give presentations. Often papers from these presentations will be published together in a book.

3. Importance of U.S. government documents. In science and technology fields the federal government plays a large role. Research and development in any field requires equipment, facilities, and funding, something the federal government can provide. Further, enforcement of safety standards for the common good requires government involvement. As a result, a lot of government departments conduct research and produce thousands of research reports every year. Many of them are very relevant to students in science and technology fields. The Department of Agriculture, for instance, conducts studies, develops land use policies, and manages the food stamp program. The Department of Defense is heavily involved in advancing aviation and navigation technology. The Department of Health and Human Services contains the Food and Drug Administration, which determines which food and drug products are available to consumers. The Department of Labor develops and enforces OSHA and NIOSH safety regulations. The Department of Transportation sets regulations for aviation and investigates transportation accidents. The EPA has played quite a role in developing and enforcing corporate pollution regulations. All these organizations produce reports and other publications which are received by many university libraries.

The federal government also sponsors much of the research that is conducted in universities and research centers around the country. The government provides grant funding for the research to be completed. In return, the grant recipient provides the government with a copy of the final research report. These quasi-government documents *do not* come to libraries free through the depository system. They are sold by the National Technical Information Service (NTIS).

THINK ABOUT THIS. . . .

When you don't know where to go in the library, you can save a lot of time by asking at the Reference Desk. Say, for instance, you want to locate information about how global warming affects a certain kind of frog in South America. When you approach a library staff member for help, ask for what you actually want. For example, don't say, "I need information on weather and how it affects things." True, your subject deals with the weather, but it is more complicated than that. With that request, you may not get the help you need. Librarians know the library resources, and can help you, if you tell them what you want, first!

THINK ABOUT THIS....

Nothing impresses a prospective employer or faculty advisor more than a student or prospective employee who can chat knowledgeably about his or her field. This shows initiative, personal interest in the field, and intelligence. This is what you need to do to become knowledgeable:

1. Identify a handful of periodicals in your field. They should range from newsy magazines to a couple of scholarly journals. A faculty member or professional in your field can assist you.

2. Sit down each month with new issues of these titles. Scan the headlines. Read the articles that interest you. Look at the advertisements. In the scholarly journals read the abstracts (summaries) at the beginning of each article. By doing this, not only do you absorb knowledge in your field, but you benefit indirectly in ways you might not have anticipated. You will find it much easier to select topics for papers, as you will know what kinds of articles are out there. You will also become more comfortable with the library, and will be able to locate resources more easily.

What is a Research Report?

At times research will be published in the form of a research report. Research or technical reports abound in science and technology fields. Research reports are not journal articles, although they usually focus on a narrow topic like journal articles. Research reports are not books, although they are distributed individually like books. They are somewhere in between. A number of professional organizations publish research reports on behalf of their members. Often these groups will sell these reports to the public. Some organizations that publish reports are The Consumer Product Safety Commission, SAE (Society of Automotive Engineers), and the NFPA (National Fire Protection Association). Dozens of other organizations, such as local governments and police departments, issue reports. These reports can sometimes be acquired through interlibrary loan or purchased outright from the issuing organization.

The Social Sciences

The category of the social sciences, covered in Chapter 12, is extremely broad. It is defined as "disciplines...which deal with aspects of human society" (Dahrendorf, 1996). One could argue that *all* subjects are a social science because everything relates somehow to the human society. Subjects in the social sciences traditionally include anthropology, economics, geography, history, political science, psychology sociology, and education. Over the years academic disciplines have split into specializations. In this book the social sciences will include: accounting, computer office systems, criminal justice, economics, education, finance, geography, marketing, legal studies, physical education, political science, psychology, recreation, sociology, social work, special education, and tourism. Notice that history and anthropology remain in the humanities. As you can see this subject area covers many

Figure 9.1

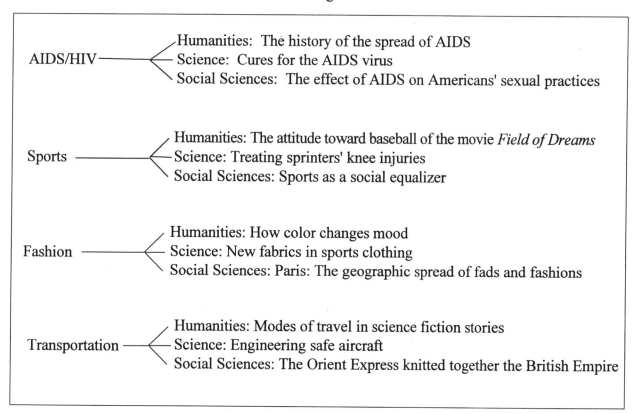

AIDS/HIV ——— Humanities: The history of the spread of AIDS
Science: Cures for the AIDS virus
Social Sciences: The effect of AIDS on Americans' sexual practices

Sports ——— Humanities: The attitude toward baseball of the movie *Field of Dreams*
Science: Treating sprinters' knee injuries
Social Sciences: Sports as a social equalizer

Fashion ——— Humanities: How color changes mood
Science: New fabrics in sports clothing
Social Sciences: Paris: The geographic spread of fads and fashions

Transportation ——— Humanities: Modes of travel in science fiction stories
Science: Engineering safe aircraft
Social Sciences: The Orient Express knitted together the British Empire

diverse topics that may not seem related in any way. However, there is a single thread of commonality—they all deal with phases of human interaction and society.

As in the sciences, researchers in the social sciences rely on journals to share current research and news of their field and government documents for a wide range of information. Unlike the sciences, however, earlier social science research is often not as rapidly or certainly replaced by current research, and social science researchers often rely on old data, artifacts, and textual material to shed light on their field of study. Social science researchers, then, will explore resources in the reference collection, in periodicals, government documents, and the book collection. They will also find a wealth of information on the Internet.

The general reference sources, like those covered in Chapter 6, may aid you in beginning your search, but to take your research one step further you should become more familiar with those sources in your particular subject field. Resources listed in Chapter 12 are only the beginning. For every one listed there are dozens of others that exist. Also keep in mind that you should not limit yourself to those sources designed for a specific subject. Sometimes there are sources for other subject-specific areas that might be useful in completing your assignments.

CASE IN POINT

Patti, a marketing major, decided to write a paper about the diamond trade. She started out only using business magazines and other business resources. After awhile she thought it would be interesting to find information on the history of diamonds. She also looked for famous crimes involving diamonds, and the geography of where diamonds are mined. After broadening her search strategies she ended up with a lot more interesting information than she had at the beginning!

Interdisciplinary Topics

Many subjects or paper topics may seem to include two areas, or even all three areas at once. For instance, history is considered by some to be part of the humanities because it deals with human experience. Others argue that it is a social science. Psychology is often claimed by all three areas. Rigid categories and definitions are not necessary as many subjects can be viewed from all three perspectives. Figure 9.1 shows how subjects can be looked at from the three categories of humanities, sciences, and social sciences. When working on a research project, one should consider using library resources in all three areas.

Reference

Dahrendorf, R. (1996). Social Science. In Kuper, A. & Kuper, J (Eds.), *The Social Science Encyclopedia* (2nd ed.). (pp. 800-802). New York: Routledge.

THE HUMANITIES

Information resources in the humanities can cover a wide number of potential subject areas. The definition of humanities has changed from decade to decade. In the 1990's the humanities are more commonly thought to include the areas of study which are "dedicated to the disciplined development of verbal, perceptual, and imaginative skills we need to understand experience" (Commission on the Humanities, p. 2). For the purposes of this text, we will consider that the disciplines within the humanities include philosophy and religion, the visual and performing arts, language, literature, communication, history, and the study of mankind (anthropology).

Almanacs

Almanacs usually include a wide variety of information and may have numerous tables or chronologies. Some major almanacs in the humanities fields are:

African-American almanac. (1994). Detroit: Gale Research.

> First published in 1967 as the *Negro Almanac*, the sixth edition called, the *African-American Almanac*, continues the tradition of the earlier work. A comprehensive reference work, it includes a chronology of important events in African-American history, a chapter of African-American Firsts, and more than 25 other topically arranged chapters of information. Topics include politics, literature, military, performing arts, civil rights, and law. Within each are short biographies of important individuals and other relevant reference information. A complete bibliography of sources referenced and a general index are at the back of the volume.

Almanac of American history. (1983). New York: Putnam.

> Arranged chronologically, each chapter is written by a scholar in American history. Within each chapter are entries on events of the period. Sidebar pieces are interspersed with a variety of biographies, definitions, and short paragraphs on a topic.

Nelson, R. F. (1981). *Almanac of American letters*. Los Altos, CA: William Kaufmann.

> A general work covering a wide range of information on the history of American literature. Chapters contain selected information chosen by the author as representative of the American literary movement. Quotations, facts and figures, banned books, pseudonyms, and anecdotes are among the chapters covered. While claiming no comprehensiveness, the work is useful to anyone studying American literature. It includes a bibliography and a general index.

Almanac of famous people. (1989). Detroit: Gale Research.

> This three-volume set offers a guide to more than 25,000 people famous and infamous from the early period of the Bible to modern times. There are chronological, geographical and occupational indexes.

Contemporary music almanac. (1980-Present). New York: Schirmer.

> An annual compilation of information related to the music business, particularly to rock music. Contains directories, calendars, lists and awards as well as biographical descriptions of musicians and musical groups.

International motion picture almanac. (1929-Present). New York: Quigley.

> Title may vary somewhat, but the contents are the same. It includes all kinds of information about the film industry and the people in it.

International television almanac. (1956-Present). New York: Quigley.

> Contains general details about actors, agencies, producers, distributors, and other common information items about television; including statistics.

World almanac book of World War II. (1981). New York: World Almanac Publications.

> Gives a chronology of events to World War II, from before the beginning of the war to the years after the war. Also has information on land, sea and air warfare, along with a casualties summary.

While it is sometimes difficult to distinguish between an almanac and a handbook or manual, the following titles may be considered humanities almanacs.

Backstage handbook: An illustrated almanac of technical information.

The black almanac.

The fantasy almanac.

The hodgepodge book.

The literary life: A scrapbook almanac of the Anglo-American literary scene form 1900 to 1950.

Atlases

Although atlases are not so frequently thought of as resources in the humanities, there are quite a number of them available.

Atlas for anthropology. (1968). Dubuque, IA: William C. Brown.

> Designed to aid those enrolled in introductory courses in anthropology, this atlas provides maps which indicate tribal and ethnic groups for the world and includes language families, human fossil locations, and the racial distribution of humans.

Atlas of classical history. (1985). New York: Macmillan.

> Covers the classical history of the world from 6500 B.C. through the time of Constantine. Includes information on such classical cities at Troy, Sparta, Athens, and Helicarnassus. Provides maps showing the Etruscan and Roman expansion into Gaul and Africa. Designed to be of use to the high school and undergraduate college student. Includes a gazetteer of place names indexing the maps on which they occur.

Atlas of Western art history. (1994). New York: Facts on File.

> A guide to the art and culture of the western world from ancient Greece through modern American art. Includes chapters with text on important periods and art forms such as Etruscan art, Islamic art, Venetian architecture, European furniture and furnishings. Numerous color illustrations and clearly defined maps make this a visually attractive work. Includes a general index.

Case In Point

A student is gathering material for a presentation about the different Native American languages that were once representative of the tribes that occupied the United States. He has been having difficulty identifying the various nations and where they lived, that is, until he discovered an atlas that showed various maps of Indian nations and where they made their homes during different periods of history. He then wondered if atlases existed for other things besides languages!

Atlas of world cultures. (1989). Newbury Park, CA: Sage.

> A geographical guide to books, articles, reports, archival materials, maps, and other materials of ethnographic literature of interest to anthropologists. Indicates the cultural groupings associated with each geographic region of the world. The work includes a bibliography and a culture index.

Dalby, D. (1977). *Language map of Africa and the adjacent islands*. London: International African Institute.

> Just as the name implies, it contains geographical maps to the various languages found in Africa and the surrounding islands.

Goode, C. T. & Shannon, E. F. (1976). *An atlas of English literature*. Norwood, PA: Norwood.

> Covers various periods of time. Includes table of authors.

Historical atlas of religion in America. (1976) New York: Harper and Row.

> Arranged into three chronological parts and one section on special aspects of religion in America, the major religious movements are plotted and discussed in the text. Bibliographic sources are included throughout the text. Several appendices provide statistical data on religion in America. A general index is included.

Historical atlas of the United States. (1988). Washington, DC: National Geographic Society.

> Numerous color illustrations and maps trace the history of the United States from its earliest settlement. The maps show economic, cultural, and historical events as they unfold during the decades covered. Interesting historical facts are included in each section providing a resource for American historical trivia.

Rand McNally and Company. (1965). *Atlas of world history*. Chicago: Rand McNally.

> Good color maps for events primarily during the 19th and 20th centuries.

Rand McNally Bible atlas. (1962). Chicago: Rand McNally.

> More for the general reader than for the scholar. Many illustrations and maps, along with a geographical and place-name index.

Additional atlases include the following titles:

Atlas of American history.

An atlas of fantasy.

Atlas historique de la musique.

Atlas of modern Jewish history.

Atlas of the Bible.

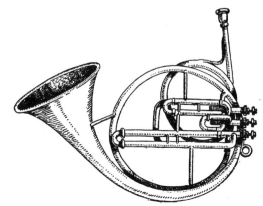

Atlas of World War I.

The linguistic atlas of England.

Urban atlas: 20 American cities; a communication study.

Bibliographies

General and subject specific bibliographies abound in libraries. You can find a bibliography published for almost anything!

Art books, 1959-1979. (1979). New York: Bowker.

> Lists more than 35,000 books. Subsequent editions follow.

Beaumont, C. W. (1929). *A bibliography of dancing*. London: Dancing Times.

> Annotated with a subject index.

A bibliography of contemporary linguistic research. (1978). New York: Garland Publishing.

> A tool to be used for those studying, teaching, or researching in the field of linguistics. Includes textbooks and popular works, anthologies and collections such as conference reports, doctoral theses and dissertations, and monographic works in the field. Arranged alphabetically by title, there is a language index and a subject index.

Blum, E. (1980). *Basic books in the mass media*. Urbana, IL: University of Illinois Press.

> Arranged according to broad subject area such as broadcasting, journalism, advertising, book publishing, and others.

Dyment, A. R. (1975). *The literature of the film: A bibliographical guide to the film as art and entertainment*. New York: White Lion.

> Annotated work of books (in English) from the 1930's to the date given in the title. Over 1,300 entries.

Floyd, S. A. & Reisser, M. J. (1983). *Black music in the United States: An annotated bibliography of selected reference and research materials*. New York: Kraus International Publishers.

> Listing of all kinds of reference sources [Online]. Available: dictionaries, biographical sources, indexes, etc.

Freeman, J. (1990). *Books kids will sit still for*. New York: Bowker. **and**

More books kids will sit still for. (1995). Providence, NJ: Bowker.

> Subtitled a read-aloud guide, the companion volumes include a manual on reading aloud, booktalking, storytelling, and the celebration of children's books for teachers, school and public librarians, parents, and anyone with children in preschool through the sixth grade. Annotated listings of children's literature are arranged by category and age level. Each volume has author, title, and subject indexes.

Iwaschkin, R. (1986). *Popular music: A reference guide*. New York: Garland Publishing.

> Lists resources for popular musical works grouped by type of music. Published primarily in the English language including country, folk, jazz, black, and Cajun, as well as the biographical and descriptive literature about these types of music.

The literature of theology: A guide for students and pastors. (1979). Philadelphia: Westminster Press.

> Need an article, book or other academic information? This is the source for you. Arranged by topic with an author/title index.

Magill, F. N. (1979). *Magill's bibliography of literary criticism: Selected sources for the study of more than 2,500 outstanding works of western literature.* Englewood Cliffs, NJ: Salem Press.

> The title says it all.

Perry, N. L. (1994). *The taming of the shrew: An annotated bibliography.* New York: Garland Publishing.

> One of a number of publications of bibliographies of materials on works by Shakespeare, this volume includes criticism, sources, studies, bibliographies, editions, stage histories, and adaptations all dealing with the play. There is a general index.

Recently published articles. (1976). Ottawa: Canadian Historical Association.

> Published every four months and provides international coverage. Arranged by country.

The reader's adviser. (1994). Providence, NJ: Bowker.

> A five volume reference work which includes the best sources for literature, social sciences, history, the arts, philosophy, religion, science, technology, and medicine. An excellent general reference tool for those searching for resources for any of the broad subjects covered.

Taylor, T. J. (1992). *American theatre history.* Pasadena, CA: Salem Press.

> An annotated bibliography of works on the history of the American stage, including both dramatic and musical theater. One of the volumes in the *Magill Bibliographies* series. Covers ethnic, academic, community and children's theater as well as successful commercial ventures on and off-Broadway.

Tischler, A. (1988). *A descriptive bibliography of art music by Israeli composers.* Warren, MI: Harmonie Park Press.

> Arranged alphabetically by names of Israeli composers, the work includes a brief biographical entry followed by a bibliography of the composer's works. A volume of the *Detroit Studies in Music Bibliography*, it is intended to encourage the performance and study of the works listed.

Here are some other bibliographies you may wish to review.

African music: A bibliographical guide.

American choral music Since 1920: An annotated guide.

Annotated bibliographies for anthropologists.

British theatre: A bibliography, 1901 to 1985.

Historical sciences, philosophy and religion.

King John: An annotated bibliography.

Multicultural picture books: Art for understanding others.

Piano music by black women composers: A catalog of solo and ensemble works.

Scandinavian mythology: An annotated bibliography.

Walford's guide to reference material. Vol. 2, social and religious information sources.

Biographical Works

Biographical materials may have short sketches or more lengthy articles on individuals.

American magazine journalists, 1900-1960. (1994). Detroit: Gale Research.

> An alphabetic listing of moderately lengthy biographies (up to ten pages) with selected bibliographies of the individual's works and their photographs. Other illustrations are also included. This work is but one volume in the series *Dictionary of Literary Biography*.

Baker, T. (1984). *Baker's biographical dictionary of musicians*. New York: Schirmer Books.

> Brief biographies and bibliographies for musicians in all kinds of music fields from classical to rock.

Cummings, P. (1994). *Dictionary of contemporary American artists*. New York: St. Martin's Press.

> Primarily a source for short biographical sketches, but also includes a directory of museums, schools, and institutions that have works by the artists and galleries which represent the artists. A list of the illustrations used in the book with descriptive information for each is another interesting feature.

Great lives from history: American women series. (1995). Pasadena, CA: Salem Press.

> One of six published sets of biographical information on the lives, careers, and achievements of prominent individuals, this five-volume work includes biographies for more than 400 notable women.

Great writers of the English language. (1979). New York: St. Martin's Press.

> Sample representation of authors from past to present. Includes biographical information and a bibliography of the author's works.

Lents, H. M. (1994). *Heads of states and governments*. Jefferson, NC: McFarland.

> An alphabetical listing of governments with biographical sketches of heads of the states and governments covering 1945-1992. Entries for each government are chronological and distinguishes between heads of state and heads of government. Includes a general index of names and states.

Stegemeyer, A. (1996). *Who's who in fashion* (3rd ed.). New York: Fairchild.

> Emphasis given to present-day designers and other people in fashion world.

Theatrical directors: A biographical dictionary. (1994). Westport, CT: Greenwood Press.

> Nearly 300 individuals known for their stage directing are profiled in a work designed for use by students and theatre generalists. Includes a chronological listing of directors and a geographic listing according to where the director's primary work was done. Includes a name index, and a play, film, and television title index.

Who's who in American art, 1995-96. (1995). New Providence, RI: Bowker.

> An annual publication which lists biographical profiles of nearly 12,000 contributors to the visual arts in the United States, Canada, and Mexico. Attempts to be as inclusive as possible, but material is submitted by the individuals or updated from previous editions. Geographic and professional indexes are included as well as a comprehensive necrology through the previous year.

Who was who in the theatre, 1912-1976. (1978). Detroit: Gale Research.

> Just as the name says, it covers actors, actresses, directors, producers, playwrights for the period of time indicated. English-speaking theatres only.

Who's who in religion. (1977). Chicago: Marquis.

> Offers information to church officials, clergy, educators, other church leaders. Contains more than 18,000 entries.

There is no lack of biographical resources in the humanities. Additional works that you might look at include:

American novelists since World War II.

American playwrights since 1945.

The concise Baker's biographical dictionary of musicians.

Contemporary poets.

Foremost women in communications.

Theatrical directors: A biographical dictionary.

Universal pronouncing dictionary of biography and mythology.

Who's who in the theatre.

Who was who in American art.

Women philosophers: A bio-critical source book.

World artists 1980-1990.

Dictionaries

Dictionaries as resources include some specialized works as well as the more common usage of the word dictionary.

Beckson, K. & Ganz, A. (1975). *Literary terms; a dictionary.* New York: Farrar, Straus and Giroux.

> Defines words, offers examples, and gives short historical background to literary terms.

Blom, E. (1971). *Everyman's dictionary of music.* New York: St. Martin's Press.

> Quick reference tool for the person who is not a musician.

Calasibetta, C. M. (1975). *Fairchild's dictionary of fashion.* New York: Fairchild.

> Need to find terminology for the fashion industry? Here you go. Covers modern and historical definitions, along with pictures and sketches.

The concise Oxford dictionary of the Christian Church. (1977). New York: Oxford University Press.

> Abridged version of the comprehensive, larger work, *The Oxford dictionary of the Christian church,* gives answers for who and what, and then refers user to sections of the larger work.

Connors, T. D. (1982). *Dictionary of mass media & communication.* New York: Longman.

> Defines terms related to the communication field including television and radio broadcasting, advertising, magazine and newspaper journalism, printing, public relations, and publishing. Aim is to assist communicators with understanding the jargon of the field.

Dictionary of American regional English. (1985-). Cambridge, MA: Belknap Press.

> Currently consists of only 2 volumes, A-C and D-H, because dictionaries take a long time to compile. The work provides definitions and history of regional colloquial usage of words and phrases. A fascinating resource for those with an interest in American folk speech.

Dictionary of philosophy. (1979). New York: St. Martin's Press.

> Includes definitions of key words and phrases and includes some biographical entries of the greatest philosophers. Heavily cross-referenced, the work includes a table of symbols and abbreviations also.

A Dictionary of superstitions. (1992). Oxford: Oxford University Press.

> Provides short explanations of superstitions such as spilling salt and Friday the thirteenth. Provides a chronology of the meanings and includes the geographic origins of superstitions.

Ellmore, R. T. (1991). *NTC's mass media dictionary*. Lincolnwood, IL: National Textbook.

> Although the work's author indicates in the preface that the book is out of date, the aim is to provide a resource of the vocabulary of writers, broadcasters, publishers, film makers, and students and teachers of these disciplines. Contains more than 20,000 definitions.

Elsevier's dictionary of cinema, sound and music. (1956). New York: Elsevier.

> Offers definitions in six languages - English, French, Spanish, Italian, Dutch and German.

Kaster, J. (1990). *Putnam's concise mythological dictionary*. New York: Putnam.

> Defines over 1,100 terms from Greek, Roman, Hindu, Hebrew, Native American, Egyptian, Chinese, and other mythologies.

The Oxford companion to the theatre. (1983). London: Oxford University Press.

> Provides definitions, historical and current, to terms used in the theatre.

Oxford English dictionary (Vols. 1-20). (1993). Oxford: Clarendon Press. 20 v.

> The second edition updates the 12 volume 1933 original OED and its 4 volume supplement with 5,000 new words. It includes the history of a word's meaning providing dates and examples of its historical usage. A classic reference work.

Seymour-Smith, C. (1986). *Dictionary of anthropology*. Boston: G.K. Hall.

> Intended for students of social and cultural anthropology and to the interested lay reader. Includes some technical terms, but emphasizes theoretical and conceptual issues. Includes cross-references to terms within articles and to direct the user to the appropriate word entry.

Strahle, G. (1995) *An early music dictionary: Musical terms from British sources, 1500-1740*. Cambridge, England: Cambridge University Press.

> Arranges each definition of a word's usage in chronological order, including a source when known. Words are cross-referenced to related or synonymous terms. Contains a bibliography of sources.

Wetterau, B. (1983). *Macmillan concise dictionary of world history*. New York: Macmillan.

> Contains a listing of people, words, places and events for world history from the beginning of time. Emphasis on U.S. history.

Look at some of the following titles:

An annotated dictionary of technical, historical, and stylistic terms relating to theatre and drama.

The dictionary of Bible and religion.

An early music dictionary: Musical terms from British sources, 1500-1740.

The new Grove dictionary of opera.

The new Grove dictionary of American music.

International dictionary of art and artists.

An international dictionary of theatre language.

The literacy dictionary: The vocabulary of reading and writing.

The Shakespeare name dictionary.

The Thames and Hudson dictionary of art and artists.

Directories

Directories may have a broad scope of information but *must* include addresses to qualify under this category.

Behrens, S. (1981). *Directory of foreign language service organizations*. Washington, DC: Center for Applied Linguistics.

> Serves as a reference guide to organizations to help educators "enrich classroom" presentations.

Directory of African-American religious bodies. (1991). Washington, DC: Howard University Press.

> Organized into nine sections preceded by an introductory essay, the directory lists religious bodies, agencies, institutions, and scholars. A separate section covers other religious bodies which have a significant African American membership. Includes a glossary of terms, historical charts, and a selected bibliography.

Directory of music faculties in colleges and universities. (1972/74-Present). New York: College Music Society.

> Need to know who teaches music where? Here you go. Broken down by state, faculty names, faculty area of interest and school.

Elmore, G.C. (1990). *The communication disciplines in higher education.* Murray, KY: Association for Communication Administration

> A reference guide to 1,508 programs which offer communication courses or degrees in the United States or in Canada. Compiled from results of a survey of institutions of higher education, it includes the number of faculty, curriculum specialties, and facilities and services available at each institution.

International directory of arts. (1995). Munich, Germany: K. G. Saur.

> An annually published directory of museums, public galleries, dealers, and associations .

Literary market place. (1940-Present). New York: Bowker.

> Directory of organizations, periodicals and publishers (including officers and key personnel) for writers. Organized by types of publications; fiction, children books, etc. and publishers.

Media personnel directory: An alphabetical guide to names, addresses, and telephone numbers of key editorial and business personnel working for over 700 United States and international periodicals. (1979). Detroit: Gale Research.

> The title says it all!

Merin, J. & Burdick, E. B. (1979). *International directory of theatre, dance and folklore festivals.* Westport, CT: Greenwood Press.

> Highlights more than 850 festivals around the world, but not in the U.S. Indexed by time, name of festival and country.

CASE IN POINT

You have just written a children's novel for an audience of children between the ages of 10-15. You know you would like for someone to read it, probably for a fee, and offer you guidelines in how to make it better. The *Literary Market Place* is the place to go to find that agent who will act as an intermediary for your manuscript.

Performing arts career directory. (1994). Detroit: Gale Research.

> Includes a databank of job opportunities but also serves as a guide for anyone interested in a career in the performing arts.

Wasserman, P. (1981). *Speakers and lecturers: How to find them*. Detroit: Gale Research.

> Helps a person locate agents, companies, associations, and other sources to find public speakers on various subjects. More than 2,000 speakers are listed, along with biographical information.

Other directories indicating the variety of sources that exist in the humanities are:

Directory of American libraries with genealogy or local history collections.

Directory of art and design faculties in colleges and universities, U.S. and Canada, 1940-95.

Directory of historic American theatres.

Funding for anthropological research.

A guide to Cuban collections in the United States.

A guide to writing programs.

Encyclopedias

Encyclopedias for the humanities frequently include the word "encyclopedia" in the title.

Encyclopedia of African-American religions. (1993). New York: Garland Publishing.

> A one volume reference work covering religious groups, leaders, and the major issues raised by the development of African American religious life. While limited to the United States, the work has a broad coverage of information and is indexed and cross-referenced.

Encyclopedia of ethics. (1992). New York: Garland Publishing.

> Two volumes of 435 signed articles covering philosophical issues of ethics. A list of the entries is included in volume one and a general index is in volume two.

Encyclopedia of Latin America. (1974). New York: McGraw-Hill.

> Comprehensive look at Central and South America. Alphabetical arrangement with cross-references.

Encyclopedia of Latin American history and culture. (1996). New York: Charles Scribner's Sons.

> Almost 5,300 signed articles provide a wide range of information on the history and culture of the area known as Latin America. Cross references are included and volume five contains a general index.

Encyclopedia of religion. (1987). New York: Macmillan.

> A multi-volume comprehensive work covering the world's religions.

Encyclopedia of social history. (1994). New York: Garland.

> A specialized one-volume work that focuses on the effect human behavior on history. Of interest to those studying both history and sociology, the work contains signed articles followed by references. Includes a general index.

Encyclopedia of world art. (1959-1983). New York: McGraw-Hill.

> Sixteen volume collection is written by specialists in the various fields. Offers good photographs and plates of art works. Articles have good bibliographies.

ICP encyclopedia of photography. (1984). New York: Crown.

> Single-volume source offers nearly 1,400 text and photographic entries. Biographical section for photographers is also included.

International encyclopedia of communications. (1989). New York: Oxford University Press.

> A four-volume set with signed articles on topics dealing with some facet of communication. Includes numerous illustrations and a thorough index.

Jablonski, E. (1981). *The encyclopedia of American music.* Garden City, NY: Doubleday.

> Includes entries for terms, works and some biographical sketches.

Jackson, G. M. (1994). *Encyclopedia of traditional epics.* Santa Barbara, CA: ABC-CLIO.

> A reference work that covers the characters, themes, and issues of the classical epic works. Includes appendices that list the epics geographically, chronologically, and by subgenre. Includes a bibliography and index.

Not all encyclopedias are multi-volume works like the *Encyclopaedia Britannica*. Others that cover subjects in the Humanities are:

The 1890's: An encyclopedia of British literature, art, and culture.

Brassey's encyclopedia of military history and biography.

The Cambridge encyclopedia of language.

Concise encyclopedia of Jewish music.

Encyclopedia of anthropology.

Encyclopedia of philosophy.

Encyclopedia of Sikh religion and culture.

The encyclopedia of the British press, 1422-1992.

Encyclopedia of the Roman empire.

Handbooks and Manuals

Ackermann, A. S. E. (1950). *Popular fallacies: A book of common errors explained and corrected, with copious references to authorities.* London: Old Westminster Press.

> Literature is viewed from a "not-true" point of view. Divided into broad headings such as food, weather, etc. with a subject index.

> ## CASE IN POINT
>
> You are listening to a radio station and the announcer indicates that he has a trivia question about movies that could win you two tickets to see your favorite rock group. The answer to that question may be easily answered if you had a copy of Halliwell's film guide, *The Complete Encyclopedia of Television Programs, 1947-1979*, or other similar source.

Allen, C. G. (1977). *A manual of European languages for librarians*. New York: Bowker.

> Gives information about languages of Europe. Subdivided by geographic sections.

Architect's handbook of professional practice. (1969). Washington, DC: American Institute of Architects.

> Three-volume work includes information, including careers, insurance, contracts, forms and other matters pertinent to someone in the profession.

Artist's & graphic designer's market. (1995). Cincinnati, OH: Writer's Digest Books.

> A directory of where and how to sell illustrations, fine art, graphic design and cartoons. Published annually it includes over 2,500 markets including magazine, book, and greeting card publishers, galleries, art publishers, and ad agencies.

Cheney, C. R. (1978). *Handbook of dates for students of English history*. London: Offices of the Royal Historical Society.

> Chronological study of English history.

French, R. D. (1947). *A Chaucer handbook*. New York: Crofts.

> Need to know information about the author or his works? Look no further!

Guinness book of music. (1981). Middlesex, England: Guinness Superlatives.

> This does for music what the *Guinness book of world records* does for general interest items. Arranged by names and instruments.

Halliwell, L. (1983). *Halliwell's film guide*. New York: Scribner.

> Alphabetical listing of films from around the world, but mainly English-language films. Not comprehensive, containing some 10,000 entries.

Handbook of American women's history. (1990). New York: Garland.

> A reference guide for information in the field of American women's history intended to assist students, teachers, and librarians. Each entry seeks to establish the historical significance of the topic covered.

Maclin, A. (1981). *Reference guide to English: A handbook of English as a second language*. New York: Holt, Rinehart and Winston.

> Serves to help non-native speakers solve language problems without consulting their instructor. Includes cross-references in a dictionary arrangement.

Magill, F. (1963). *Cyclopedia of literary characters*. New York: Harper.

> Provides information on the characters in selected works from all periods of time from the Greek empire to the modern era. Arranged by title, with an author and character index.

Munroe, M. H. & Banja, J. R. (1991). *The birthday book*. New York: Neal-Schuman Publishers.

> Handbook of birthdates, birthplaces, and sources of biographical information for American authors and illustrators of children's books.

The Oxford companion to American theatre. (1984). New York: Oxford University Press.

> A guide to the theatre as performed on the American stage, including a number of foreign plays which have influenced the American theatre. Unsigned articles range from short paragraphs to half page entries. There is no index.

The Oxford companion to Twentieth-century art. (1981). New York: Oxford University Press.

> Neither a dictionary nor an encyclopedia, this reference book is intended to serve as a handbook and guide through the world of contemporary art. Articles include biographical entries, accounts of movements and associations, definitions of special terms, and historical information. Includes color illustrations of some art works.

Terrace, V. (1979). *The complete encyclopedia of television programs, 1947-1979*. South Brunswick, NJ: A. S. Barnes.

> This is an alphabetical listing of programs from 1947 through 1979. Gives names of performers, type of show, playing time, dates televised and brief summary. This is an excellent source for the television Jeopardy player.

Writer's market: Where & how to sell what you write. (1995) Cincinnati, OH: Writer's Digest Books.

> A guide for the writer who wants to be published. Includes sections on getting started as a writer and business details every writer should consider. It provides information on the various markets available for writers. Includes a general index.

Reference handbooks and manuals can run the gamut of any reference materials that do not fall into one of the other categories of reference books. The words guide, manual, or handbook may be in the titles but are not always. Some examples:

Art career guide.

Art in the ancient world: A handbook of style and form.

The Oxford companion to American literature.

Perry's broadcast news handbook.

Indexes and Abstracts

Libraries may arrange major indexes separately from other Reference works. More concise index works are usually among the other reference materials. Some indexes also are published in electronic format.

Art index. (1929-Present). New York: H. W. Wilson.

> Published quarterly, this author/subject index to the various fields of art, archaeology, art history, crafts, graphic arts, photography, etc. It covers nearly 200 periodicals.

Contento, W. (1978). *Index to science fiction anthologies and collections*. Boston: G. K. Hall.

> Comprehensive work covering science fiction through 1977. Lists nearly 2,000 books with 12,000 different stories.

The Columbia Granger's index to poetry. (1994). New York: Columbia University Press.

Indexes poetry in collections and anthologies by title, first line, last line, author, and subject. A list of the codes for anthologies indexed with their full citations is included. The earliest edition of *Granger's Index to Poetry* dates to 1902. The work is not cumulative so all editions must be retained for comprehensive coverage.

Essay and general literature index. (1900-). New York: H. W. Wilson.

Author and subject index to literature sources in book collections. Check here to find additional information when researching any topic in the humanities or social sciences.

Film literature index. (1973-Present). New York: Filmdex.

Published quarterly with an annual cumulation, this source indexes approximately 300 periodical titles for articles concerning films. Also contains book reviews.

Humanities index. (1974-Present). New York: H. W. Wilson.

A subject and author index to English language periodical literature in the fields of archaeology and classical studies, folklore, history, language and literature, performing arts, philosophy, religion and theology. Earlier literature is indexed in the anteceding titles of the *International Index* (1907-1965) and the *Social Sciences & Humanities Index* (1966-1974).

Index to fairy tales, 1987-1992. (1994). Metuchen, NJ: Scarecrow Press.

An index to fairy tales, folktales, myths, and legends from collected works, including title, author, and subject entries. Previous cumulations cover 1916-1986. Provides sources for reviews of the collections and a code indicating the reading level of the material.

Index to Jewish periodicals. (1963-Present). Cleveland Heights, OH: Index to Jewish Periodicals.

Is published quarterly and indexes approximately forty journals, and includes book reviews.

Index to poetry for children and young people. (1964-Present). New York: H. W. Wilson.

A title, subject, author, and first line index to poetry in collections. Earlier works are indexed in the Index to *Children's Poetry and its Supplements* (1942-1965). Includes a section on the books of poetry indexed and a directory of publishers and distributors.

MLA international bibliography. (1969-Present). New York: Modern Language Association.

Published quarterly with annual cumulations, indexes books and articles on the modern languages and literature. Organized since 1980 by geographic origin of the literature and by time period. There is a subject and an author index to the listings.

Music index. (1949-Present). Warren, MI: Harmonie Park Press.

A subject and author index to musical periodical literature, published quarterly and cumulated annually.

The philosopher's index. (1967-Present). Bowling Green, OH: Philosophy Documentation Center.

A subject and author index with abstracts of philosophy books and journals in English, French, German, Spanish, and Italian, along with selected materials in other languages. Published quarterly and cumulated annually. Includes a list of periodicals indexed and a book review index. Earlier works from 1940-1976 are indexed in the *Philosopher's Index: A Retrospective Index to U.S. Publications* and *A Retrospective Index to Non-U.S. English Language Publications*.

Play index. (1949-Present). New York: H. W. Wilson.

Five year cumulative indexes to plays published individually and in collections, written or translated into English. Arranged as one author, title, and subject index with complete entry under author's name. Includes a cast analysis section for locating plays by number of players, male, female, or mixed cast, puppet cast, unidentified cast, or variable cast as well as a list of collections indexed and a directory of publishers and distributors.

Short story index. (1900-Present). New York: H. W. Wilson Company.

> Issued annually with five year cumulations and covers short stories written in or translated into English appearing in collections and selected periodicals. Arranged by author, title and subject in one alphabetical listing with the fullest entry under the author's name. Includes a list of collections indexed, a directory of publishers, and a directory of periodicals.

Quotation Books

To really impress someone with a paper or presentation, choose an appropriate quotation. Here is where many humanities-related quotations can be found.

The quotable woman, 1800-1981. (1982). New York: Facts on File.

> Quotes from women for the period of time indicated. Indexed by subject.

The quotable Shakespeare. (1988). Jefferson, NC: McFarland.

> Arranged by alphabetical topics, the work contains 6,516 quotations covering a broad scope of thoughts and emotions. A topical index allows the users to locate quotes when only a key word or idea is recalled. Includes a character and title index and each entry is assigned a sequential number for ease in identifying it on the page.

Quotations in Black. (1981). Westport, CT: Greenwood Press.

> Designed to provide a source for short quotations from people from all over the world. Includes over 1,100 quotations from more than two hundred individuals representing thirty-seven countries and ten languages. Also includes four hundred anonymous proverbs that are thought to have been spoken or written by Blacks. A subject and keyword index provide access to the numbered entries.

What they said. (1969-Present). Beverly Hills, CA: Monitor Book Company.

> Gives quotations for the given year. Divided into three sections: National Affairs, International Affairs, and an index by person and subject.

Scarborough, W. (1926). *Collection of Chinese proverbs*. Shanghai, China: Presbyterian Mission Press.

> Proverbs arranged by classification and indexed by subject.

Very specific books of quotations are also available. Among them:

Artists in quotation: A dictionary of the creative thoughts of painters, sculptors, designers, writers, educators, and others.

Feminist quotations.

Film quotations: 11,000 lines spoken on screen, arranged by subject, and indexed.

My soul looks back, 'lest I forget: A collection of quotations by people of color.

The speaker's sourcebook: Quotes, stories, and anecdotes for every occasion.

They never said it: A book of fake quotes, misquotes, and misleading attributions.

Warrior's words: a quotation book : From Sesostris III to Schwarzkopf.

Internet Resources

Internet Resources

Below are some of the many Internet sources available to you. These will give you a start in your quest for Web information, although many more are available. If titles of the sites are not self-explanatory a brief description is given.

AMARC-World Association of Community Radio Broadcasters [Online]. Available: *http://www/web/apc.org/amarc/*

American Historical Review (Journal) [Online]. Available: *http://www.indiana.edu/~amhrev/*

Ansel Adams [Online]. Available: *http://bookweb.cwis.uci.edu:8042/AdamsHome.html*

ArchiWeb-Architecture on the Internet [Online]. Available: *http://www.archiweb.com/*

Art History-Notre Dame [Online]. Available: *http://www.nd.edu/~art/arthistory.html*

At The Movies [Online]. Available: *http://webking.com/movies/index.html*

August Rodin [Online]. Available: *http://www.paris.org/Musees/Rodin/*

Central California Poetry Journal [Online]. Available: *http://www.solopublications.com/journal.htm*

Comparative Religion [Online]. Available: *http://weber.u.washington.edu/~madin/*

Dance Directory [Online]. Available: *http://www.cyberspace.com/vandehey/dance.html*

Dino-Trekking (Guide to Dinosaurs) [Online]. Available: *http://www.bridge.net/~gryphon/dino/*

Electronic Journal of Analytic Philosophy (EJAP) [Online]. Available: *http://www.phil.indiana.edu/ejap/ejap.html*

ESL (English as a Second Language) Virtual Catalog [Online]. Available: *http://www.pvp.com/esl.htm*

Guide to Theater Resources on the Internet [Online]. Available: *http://www.ircam.fr/divers/theatre-e.html*

History-WWW Virtual Library [Online]. Available: *http://history.cc.ukans.edu/history/WWW_history_main.html*

Internet Resources

Horus' History Links (Over 1700 links to history resources) [Online]. Available: http://www.ucr.edu/h-gig/horuslinks.html

Humanities-WWW Virtual Library [Online]. Available: *http://www.hum.gu.se/w3vl/ w3vl.html*

HUMBUL Gateway to International Humanities Resources [Online]. Available: http://info.ox.ac.uk/departments/humanities/international.html

Internet Philosophy Resources [Online]. Available: *http://www.philo.mcgill.ca/*

Internet Television Resource Guide [Online]. Available: *http://www.teleport.com/ ~celinec/tv.shtml*

Languages Virtual Library [Online]. Available: http://www.willamette.edu/~tjones/ languages/WWW_Virtual_Library_*Language.html*

Links to Ancient History [Online]. Available: *http://www.ghgcorp.com/shetler/*

Multimedia and ClipArt [Online]. Available: *http://www.itec.sfsu.edu/multimedia/ multimedia.html*

Music-WWW Virtual Library [Online]. Available: *http://syy.oulu.fi/music/*

National Press Club [Online]. Available: *http://npc.press.org/*

Newbie's Guide to Music [Online]. Available: *http://ug.cs.dal.ca:3400/music.html*

Religion and Philosophy Resources on the Internet [Online]. Available: *http:// web.bu.edu/STH/Library/contents.html*

Table of Faiths (Religions of the World) [Online]. Available: http:// www.servtech.com/public/mcroghan/religion.htm

Vincent van Gogh (1853-1890) [Online]. Available: *http://hops.cs.jhu.edu/~baker/ van_gogh.html*

References

Commission on the Humanities. (1980). *The humanitites in Ameri-can life*. Berkeley, CA: University of California Press.

THE SCIENCES

This chapter covers specialized resources for students doing research in the sciences, both pure and applied. Science topics include (but are not limited to): agriculture, automotive technology, aviation, child development, construction, dietetics, electronics technology, fashion merchandising, graphics, home economics, hospitality management, industrial hygiene, industrial management, manufacturing, military science, nursing, power mechanics, safety science, and textiles and clothing. Pure science topics include biology, chemistry, computer science, earth science, geology, mathematics, physics, and zoology.

Specialized library resources can largely be categorized as they were in Chapter 6. The following categories will be used:

Almanacs   Directories
Atlases   Encyclopedias
Bibliographies   Handbooks and Manuals
Biographical Works   Industrial Standards
Dictionaries

Almanacs

An almanac will provide up-to-date lists and statistics from a large variety of sources. They can lead you to more in-depth resources.

Aviation & aerospace almanac. (1993). Washington, DC: McGraw-Hill.

> Contains more than one million facts, figures, names and numbers covering the entire aviation and aerospace industries. The user must consult the table of contents for data included as there is no index to the work.

Bunch, B. *(1992). Timetables of technology: A chronology of the most important people and events in the history of technology.* New York: Simon & Schuster.

> Scientific and technological inventions and discoveries from throughout history are organized in tables under such headings as communication, transportation, tools, and food. Information is indexed by year, subject and name.

Internet Resources

Computer Almanac - Interesting and Useful Numbers about Computers. [Online].
URL http://www.cs.cmu.edu/afs/cs.cmu.edu/user/bam/www/numbers.html

Just how many people today own computers? What are the current estimates on the number
of people using the world wide web? These types of questions are answered through a series of
links to such estimations.

Rutkowski, A.M. Internet Trends. [WWW page]. URL http://www.genmagic.com/
internet/trends/

This site concentrates on Internet statistics. It provides numbers on the present number of
hosts and sites per three-litter domain.

Atlases

The Cambridge atlas of astronomy (3rd ed.). (1994). New York: Cambridge University Press.

This atlas does more than show pictures of solar systems and galaxies. Its text, tables and diagrams explain the
composition and behavior of celestial bodies.

Rand McNally commercial atlas and marketing guide. (1978-). Chicago: Rand McNally, Annual.

This atlas provides maps of each state depicting various economic features, such as manufacturing areas and railroads.
Since it is reissued annually, the information can be counted on being up-to-date.

Bibliographies

Aluri, R. & Robinson, J. S. (1983). *A guide to U.S. government scientific and technical resources.*
Littleton, CO: Libraries Unlimited.

Don't let the date of this resource bother you. It describes the type of information available from the federal government
and how to access it.

Hurt, C. D. (1994). *Information sources in science and technology* (2nd ed.). Englewood, CO: Libraries Unlimited.

This book lists reference resources in the science and technology fields. It is arranged somewhat like this chapter,
organizing the resources by type, such as almanacs, dictionaries, etc.

Malinowsky, H. R. (1994). *Reference sources in science, engineering, medicine, and agriculture.*
Phoenix: The Oryx Press.

This guide can help you find information sources for a research project. It lists over 2,000 works in nine chapters.

Other bibliographies:

*Electronic campus, electronic classroom, electronic library: An an-
notated bibliography.*

Women in agriculture: A guide to research.

Biographical Works

American men & women of science: A biographical directory of today's leaders in physical, biological and related sciences (19th ed., Vols. 1-8). (1995-96). New Providence, NJ: R. R. Bowker.

This edition contains biographical information about 123,406 living scientists. Older editions are kept in the library for access to deceased scientists. Each entry contains such information as date of birth, education, jobs held, research information, awards won, and present address. New in this edition is the option for an email address.

Biographical dictionary of scientists (2nd ed.). (1994). New York: Oxford University Press.

While the other biographical resources listed here simply list important information, this work has written articles, like an encyclopedia. It includes people both alive and deceased.

Stegemeyer, A. (1996). *Who's who in fashion* (3rd ed.). New York: Fairchild Publications.

This is information that is otherwise hard to find. It provides short articles about designers, both historical figures and newcomers to the field. Most entries include a picture of the designer or an example of his or her work, or both.

Who's who in technology (6th ed., Vols. 1-2). (1989). Detroit, MI: Gale Research.

This source contains information on 38,000 people. It includes people who have contributed to science and technology through publications, special achievements, and positions of responsibility in businesses and organizations shaping their fields.

Dictionaries

Science and technology fields are filled with special terms and jargon. Dictionaries can be very important.

Courvisier, A. (1994). *A dictionary of military history and the art of war* (English Rev. Ed.), Childs, J. (Ed.) & C. Turner, Trans.). Cambridge, MA: Blackwell. (Original work published 1988).

Rather than arranging the information as a list of battles, the editor chose to focus on themes and emphasize the relationship between armed forces and the society they represent. The authored articles are long, academic in style, and often include references for further reading. An excellent resource for the study of the military. The enlarged edition has new material, including interesting examples psychological warfare used during the Gulf War.

Firesmith, D. G. (1995). *Dictionary of object technology: The definitive desk reference.* New York: SIGS Books.

The computer reference material in a library must be constantly updated to keep up with advancements. This dictionary sets to record the usage of terminology among object-oriented programmers. The authors recognize the inconsistencies in the language, and hope that their work will speed its development.

Gary, M. (1973). *Glossary of geology.* Washington, DC: American Geological Institute.

This work is from the authoritative source, the American Geological Institute. It contains almost 33,000 entries which attempt to standardize the usage of geological terminology in the field. Many definitions contain citations to an important work on that subject.

Illustrated encyclopedia of general aviation (2nd ed.). (1990). Blue Ridge Summit, PA: TAB Books.

Although its called an encyclopedia, it is more like a dictionary because it has short definitions of aviation terms. It contains numerous pictures and charts.

Internet Resources

BABEL - A Glossary of Computer-oriented Abbreviations & Acronyms. [Online].
Available: http://www.access.digex.net/~ikind/babel.html
This large dictionary lists thousands of computer and Internet related abbreviations and acronyms.

Markus, J. & Sclater, N. (1994). *McGraw-Hill electronics dictionary* (5th ed.). New York: McGraw-Hill.

This is an excellent dictionary for electronics. It covers 14,000 terms and has 1,500 illustrations. If you don't find what you want, try the similar *Illustrated Dictionary of Electronics* (1993) by Stan Gibilisco (Blue Ridge Summit, PA: TAB Books).

McGraw-Hill dictionary of scientific and technical terms (5th ed.). (1994). New York: McGraw-Hill.

This book is huge, but it would have to be to cover the scope of science and technology. Over three pages in the beginning list all the subject fields covered, from "acoustics" to "zoology." It contains 122,600 definitions and has approximately 3,000 illustrations in the wide outside margins.

Mosby's medical, nursing, and allied health dictionary (3rd ed.). (1990). St. Louis: Mosby.

This is a good medical dictionary for nursing students, as it provides nearly 2,000 illustrations and "nursing considerations" for over 1,000 entries. Nineteen appendices in the back provide basic reference values for calculation.

Newton, H. (1994). *Newton's telecom dictionary: The official dictionary of computer telephony, telecommunications, networking, data communications, voice processing and the Internet.* 8th ed. N.Y: Flatiron Publishing.

This annual tries to keep pace with the constant change in the computer and telecommunications field. The definitions are understandable; they read just the way a regular person talks.

Patton-Hulce, V. (1995). *Environment and the law: A dictionary.* Santa Barbara, CA: ABC-CLIO.

For researchers wanting a general knowledge of environmental law, this dictionary is very useful. An introductory chapter overviews the development of environmental legislation. The lengthy definitions cross-reference to others in the book. A few dozen of the most important cases, laws, and regulations are cited in definitions and listed in the back.

Skelly, C. J. (1994). *Dictionary of herbs, spices, seasonings, and natural flavorings.* New York: Garland.

Around the world a common plant can be known by a long list of different names. This dictionary attempts to put order to this by providing each plant's scientific name, plus local names. The definitions focus on culinary applications for the plants rather than medicinal. Two large appendices group plants by Family and Genera.

Stein, J. Stewart. (1993). *Construction glossary: An encyclopedic reference and manual* (2nd ed.). New York: John Wiley & Sons.

This dictionary contains over 30,000 entries. They are arranged alphabetically within sixteen categories. For this reason, it is best accessed by the index. There are other construction dictionaries, some illustrated, but this one defines the most terms.

Taber's cyclopedic medical dictionary (17th ed.). (1993). Philadelphia: F. A. Davis.

In addition to definitions, this helpful dictionary provides information on the history of terms, synonyms, and pronunciations. For medical conditions, it lists symptoms, causes, treatments, prognoses, and nursing implications.

Internet Resources

ChemExper Co. ChemExper Chemical Directory. [Online]. Available: URL http://www.chemexper.be/

A directory of chemical suppliers. Search for a chemical and find a supplier. .

Thomas Register of American Manufacturers. [Online]. Available: URL http:/www.thomasregister.com:8000/home.html.

This site requires free registration for use. This is one of the few Internet sites that provides the full product as it is available in paper form. The company receives its income from manufacturers for inclusion.

The VNR dictionary of environmental health and safety. (1994). New York: Van Nostrand Reinhold.

Each of the 7,000 entries is contributed by one of ten experts in the fields of environmental law, hazardous waste, epidemiology, and industrial hygiene.

Other dictionaries include:

Computer dictionary.

Cooper's pocket environmental compliance dictionary.

Dictionary of organic compounds.

Encyclopedic dictionary of technical terms. English/Spanish Spanish/English.

Illustrated cosmetology dictionary.

Directories

The Complete drug reference. (1991). Yonkers, NY: Consumer Reports Books.

Like the Physician's Desk Reference, this resource contains information about drugs. This guide, though, is designed for consumers. It includes information about non-prescription drugs. Two appendices contain a Pregnancy Precaution Listing and Athlete's Precautions.

Index and directory of industry standards (12th ed., Vols. 1-2). (1995). Englewood, CO: Global Professional.

Numerous organizations create industrial standards. This two volume set serves as a subject index to standards.

Norback, C. T. (1989). *Hazardous chemicals on file* (Updated ed., Vols. 1-3). New York: Facts on File.

Provides formula, exposure limits, health hazard information, first-aid procedures, and waste disposal information.

Physician's desk reference. (1946-). Oradell, NJ: Medical Economics.

This work is a common sight in both doctors' offices and library reference areas. It contains product information for all FDA-approved prescription drugs. They can be accessed by product name, generic name, manufacturers, or a color picture of the pill. The information provided includes what each drug is, how to use it, warnings, and possible side effects.

Thomas' register of American manufacturers and Thomas' register catalog file (Vols 1-29). (1910-). New York: Thomas.

> This set is used in libraries and corporations across the country. The distinctive large green volumes serve as a "yellow pages" to industry. It is used to find manufacturers or distributors of products, from abacuses to zoo equipment. The last ten volumes contain company advertisements, literature, and catalogs.

World aviation directory. (1940 -). Washington, DC: World Aviation Directory. Semiannual.

> This guide consists of three parts in three volumes. The first is a directory of companies that manufacture, operate, and maintain aviation-related products and services. The second is a buyer's guide that serves as a "yellow pages" to products and services. The third is a catalog guide offering company literature, brochures, and catalogs.

Other directories include:

Directory of statistical microcomputer software.

Gale directory of databases.

Guide to college programs in hospitality and tourism.

Missouri directory of manufacturers.

Encyclopedias

Bisio, A. & Boots, S. (Eds.). (1995). *Encyclopedia of energy technology and the environment* (Vols. 1-4). New York: John Wiley & Sons.

> This encyclopedia is intended for both scientists and citizens. Each long article is written by an expert in the field. Each article contains a long list of journal articles, books and technical reports for further reference.

Concise encyclopedia chemistry (English language ed.). (1994). New York: Walter de Gruyter.

> This could better be described as an encyclopedic dictionary. It contains 12,000 entries from general, organic, inorganic, physical and technical chemistry. The articles are generally short, or concise.

Encyclopedia of agricultural science (Vols. 1-4). (1994). San Diego, CA: Academic Press.

> This is the only modern encyclopedia covering agricultural science in general available today. Its long in-depth articles provide pictures and tables that provide valuable supplementary information. Each article is written by experts in the field. At the end of each article is a list of further materials.

Encyclopedia of human biology (Vols. 1-8). (1991). San Diego, CA: Academic Press.

> This encyclopedia contains much more in-depth medical information, pictures and diagrams than a general encyclopedia can provide. It is still appropriate for the average college student, because it provides definitions to some of the more technical terms in each article. At the end of each article is a list of books and journal articles for more information.

Encyclopedia of materials science and engineering (Vols. 1-8). (1986). Cambridge, MA: MIT Press.

> This encyclopedia covers materials used in any area of industrial or mechanical engineering, and their uses and properties. Each article is written by an expert in the field and has a list for further reading at the end.

Internet Resources

National Institute of Standards and Technology. CODATA Recommended Values of the Fundamental Physical Constants. Journal of Research of the National Bureau of Standards [Online]. 92, 85-95 (1987). Available: *http://physics.nist.gov/PhysRefData/codata86/codata86.html*

Need to know the length of a Compton wavelength? The mass of an electron? These figures are available here.

Encyclopedia of the American military: Studies of the history, traditions, policies, institutions, and roles of the armed forces in war and peace (Vols. 1-3). (1994). New York: Charles Scribner's Sons.

Not only does this encyclopedia cover various engagements and activities of the military, it covers such topics as "The Socialization of the Armed Forces," and the relationship of the military to other parts of the federal government such as the presidency, legislature, and judiciary.

Ensminger, M. (1994). *Foods & nutrition encyclopedia* (2nd ed., Vols. 1-2). Boca Raton, FL: CRC Press.

This work contains information about foods and nutrition, and it includes common pharmaceuticals, mostly herbs and other common plants. It also provides information on diseases caused by malnutrition and imbalanced diets.

Grzimek's encyclopedia of mammals (Vols. 1-5). (1989). New York: McGraw-Hill.

Arranges mammals by subclass and order. It provides detailed information with a color photo of each animal. The index in each volume must be checked because there is no general index.

Other encyclopedias include:

Encyclopedia of North American birds.

Encyclopedia of physical science and technology.

Encyclopedia of statistical science.

Encyclopedia of the horse.

Handbooks and Manuals

CRC handbook of chemistry and physics: A ready-reference book of chemical and physical data. (1913-). Boca Raton, FL: CRC Press.

This book contains important data needed in chemistry and physics presented in tables and lists. It has properties and constants for organic compounds, inorganic compounds, fluid properties, atomic, molecular, nuclear, and particle physics.

Flynn. P. (1995). *The world wide web handbook: An HTML guide for users, authors and publishers.* London: International Thomson Computer Press.

Although books on the World Wide Web become quickly dated, this book is still relevant. It explains what the Web is, how to create a Web document, and what responsibilities come with it.

McGraw-Hill's national electrical code handbook (21st ed.). (1993). New York: McGraw-Hill.

> This handbook has a new edition every time the NFPA XX (ANSI/NFPA XX) is updated. It explains the standard and provides implementation instructions.

Metals handbook (9th ed., Vols. 1-17). (1978-1989). Materials Park, OH: American Society for Metals.

> Each volume has a separate topic relating to metals. Each volume treats its subject in great detail. Contains technical information, statistical information, and diagrams for metals from their basic properties, through manufacturing processes to quality control.

Handbooks exist for every topic conceivable. Below are just some:

A manual for authors of mathematical papers.

AIP style manual.

Handbook of data management.

The Madison Avenue handbook.

The scientist's handbook for writing papers and dissertations.

Writing in technical fields: A step-by-step guide for engineers, scientists, and technicians.

Indexes and Abstracts

Journal and magazine indexes and abstracts are very important for people researching in science and technology. As mentioned earlier, this is the place to find the most recent publications in your field. Indexes provide access to journals, magazines, research reports, and sometimes book chapters.

Applied science & technology index [book form] (1958-1982). [CD-ROM] (1983-present). New York: H. W. Wilson.

> This comprehensive database indexes almost 400 journals covering aeronautics, all areas of engineering, fire safety, textiles, and more. Its menu-driven searching makes it easy to use.

Biological abstracts [book form]. (1926-1992). Philadelphia: BioSciences Information Service, Semi-monthly. [Online] (1990-present). Palo Alto, CA: Dialog Information Services.

> This is the standard index in the natural sciences. Its massive size makes it much more manageable in electronic form. This index is for in-depth and high level research. One should begin with the Biological & Agricultural Index listed below.

Biological & agricultural index [book]. (1964-1982). [CD-ROM]. (1983-present). New York: H. W. Wilson.

> This index covers most areas of the natural sciences, such as botany, biology, and zoology. It is not as comprehensive as Biological Abstracts, but is more accessible and easier to use. It is a good starting point for research in these fields.

Chemical abstracts. (1907-). Columbus, OH: American Chemical Society, Weekly.

> This comprehensive index includes journal articles from 50 languages. Its huge size makes it much more manageable in electronic format. It is for in-depth research. A student should begin with the Applied Science & Technology Index before using this.

CAT/PAC plus. (1976-present). [CD-ROM]. San Antonio, TX: Marcive.

> This product indexes all U.S. government documents published by the Government Printing Office from 1976 to the present. It also indicates which items a library receives.

Occupational safety and health on CD (OSH-ROM) [CD-ROM]. (1987-). Boston: Silverplatter Information Services.

> The disk actually contains four databases. Here you will find citations to U.S. and international journal articles and technical reports in all areas of safety science and industrial hygiene.

SAE technical literature abstracts. (1985-present). Warrendale, PA: Society of Automotive Engineers.

> This paper index contains references to SAE technical reports. Most of these reports would not be owned by the library. They are available for purchase or can be borrowed through interlibrary loan.

U.S. government periodicals index [CD-ROM]. (1993-present). Bethesda, MD: CIS.

> The U.S. government publishes close to two hundred journals and magazines in many subject areas. They are all indexed here.

Other indexes exist that can help with various fields. These include:

General Science Index.

Geographical Abstracts: Physical Geography.

Mineralogical abstracts.

Standards

Occasionally in some science and technology coursework, students will run across references to industry standards. Standards are a set of statements about a product or process agreed upon by a group. They can refer to the product's performance, size, color, taste, consistency, or any other definable characteristic. Standards are set so that manufacturers and consumers alike understand what a product is and how it will work. Most electrical appliances in the United States, for instance, are developed to run on 110 volts. The power company supplies the electricity, builders install wiring to

---

THINK ABOUT THIS...

Think about all the things you buy at a store to use with things you already own. The socket of an extension cord fits right into the prongs on your appliances. A CD that you bought in one store fits right into your CD player which was purchased at another store. The threads on a 3/16" screw are spaced the same as ones you bought last year. Think what a hassle it would be if these things didn't match up. Well, actually some things do not conform to standards. Clothing, especially women's, is based very loosely on measurements developed in the 1940's. Clothing sizes are not standardized. If they were, you would wear the same size regardless of the brand. Sizes are roughly similar, but they are not standardized.

handle it, and manufacturers make products that use it. This standardization benefits everyone; manufacturers know that everyone is able to use their product, and consumers know that all products will work in their home.

> Standards and specifications are an essential part of technology, serving, for example, to minimize disadvantageous diversity, to ensure acceptability of products, to facilitate technical communication and to aid in research. *(Encyclopedia of Materials Science and Engineering*, p. 4579.)

Standards are generally developed by professional organizations, whether on an *adhoc* basis or in response to a governmental need. Standards are initially voluntary, developed for use by interested parties. Some standards, however, have been adopted by governmental bodies and are enforced as regulations.

A variety of bodies participate in developing standards, such as trade associations (Underwriters Laboratories, ASTM, SAE, ASSE) and government departments. In the United States, the American National Standards Institute (ANSI) does not write standards, but coordinates standard development among organizations and promotes general acceptance of the basic standards. The international body that serves this same function is the International Standards Organization (ISO) based in Geneva, Switzerland. It works for consensus between countries. Two issues receiving particular attention today are the transfer of digital data (ANSI Z39.50) and quality standards for suppliers (ISO 9000).

Most libraries do not buy all standards. To find out which organization developed a standard on a particular topic, consult the *Index and Directory of Industry Standards*. Consult the online catalog to find out if the library owns standards from that organization. Finally, find the standards on the shelf and locate the one needed.

Index and directory of industry standards (12th ed., Vols. 1-2). (1995). Englewood, CO: Global Professional Publications.

> This index provides access to the numerous organizations that publish standards. It will provide the appropriate standard number for each object or procedure and contact information for the organization that produces it.

American National Standards Institute. (1941-). *ANSI: American national standards*. New York: The Institute.

> ANSI is the coordinating organization for all U.S. standard-developing bodies. Not all industry standards are accepted and distributed by ANSI. ANSI distributes thousands of standards, all listed in the paper index and on ANSI's World Wide Web page. Standards can either be purchased from ANSI or from the issuing organization. Standards are not updated on any particular schedule. Each one is updated when concerned parties feel it needs to be.

Internet Resources

American National Standards Institute. [Online]. Available: http://www.ansi.org/cat_top.html

Yahoo Standards Page. http://www.yahoo.com/Reference/Standards/

> This page provides access to many standards organizations' web pages, including ANSI and ISO.

American Society of Agricultural Engineers. (1984-). *ASAE standards: Standards, engineering practices, and data adopted by the American Society of Agricultural Engineers*. St. Joseph, MI: The Association. Annual.

American Society for Testing and Materials. *Annual book of ASTM standards* (Vols. 1-70). (1970-). Philadelphia, PA: The Association. Annual.

National Fire Protection Association. (1938-). *National fire codes* (Vols. 1-13). Boston: The Association. Continuously updated.

SAE handbook (Vols. 1-3). (1924-). New York: Society of Automotive Engineers.

References

Standardization. (1992). R. McHenry (Ed.), *Encyclopaedia Britannica* (Vol. 11, p. 209). Chicago: Encyclopaedia Britannica.

Westbrook, J. H. Standards and Specifications for Materials. (1986). M. B. Bever (Ed.), *Encyclopedia of Materials Science and Engineering* (Vol. 6, pp. 4579-4585). Cambridge, MA: MIT Press.

Internet Resources

The Association for Research and Enlightenment (ARE) [Online]. Available: http://www.are-cayce.com/

The international headquarters of the work of Edgar Cayce, considered the most documented psychic of all time. Test your ESP powers.

Aviation Accident Database [Online]. Available: http://web.inter.nl.net/users/H.Ranter/frames.htm

This site is busy and inefficient, but it presents a large database of information on airplane crashes from 1970 to the present.

Internet Resources

Chaos Introduction [Online]. Available: http://www.students.uiuc.edu/~ag-ho/chaos/ chaos.html

Overview with emphasis on thought processes over actual mathematical theory.

Distance between two locations [Online]. Available: http://www.indo.com/distance/

Uses the Geographic Name Server to find the latitude and longitude of two places, and the distance between them (as the crow flies).

Earth from Space [Online]. Available: http://earth.jsc.nasa.gov/

Space shuttle earth observations photography database of over 250,000 images. Images are extremely memory intensive and require a high resolution computer monitor.

History of Computer Graphics [Online]. Available: http://www.disney.com/DisneyVideos/ ToyStory/about/history/history.htm

Excepted from the book, "Becoming a Computer Animator" by Michael Morrison. This information is part of the Toy Story web pages.

In Search of Giant Squid [Online]. Available: http://seawifs.gsfc.nasa.gov/ OCEAN_PLANET/HTML/squid_opening.html

Based upon material presented in the Smithsonian's National Museum of Natural History's exhibit "In Search of Giant Squids".

International Crop Circle Database [Online]. Available: http://rainbow.medberry.com/ enigma/1996DBase.html

John W. Mauchly and the Development of the ENIAC Computer. An Exhibition in the Department of Special Collections Van Pelt Library, University of Pennsylvania [Online]. Available: http://www.library.upenn.edu/special/gallery/mauchly/ jwmintro.html

LlamaWeb [Online]. Available: http://www.llamaweb.com/entry.html

Provides information about llamas includes pointers to llama farms, a veterinary information resource area, and llama related services.

Public Broadcasting Service. Triumph of the Nerds [Online]. Available: http:// www.pbs.org/nerds/

A companion Web site for the PBS television special. This excellent site focuses on the development of the personal computer.

The Society for Scientific Exploration [Online]. Available: http://www.jse.com/

provide a professional forum for presentations, criticism and debate concerning topics which are ingored or studied inadequately within mainstream science

Tidal Information Page [Online]. Available: http://www.catalina.org/goodies/tides.htm

Get current tides and all high and low tides for the next two weeks for over 300 harbors, beaches, inlets, river mouths, and capes around the world.

THE SOCIAL SCIENCES

This chapter covers subject-specific materials for students completing reseach in the broad category of social sciences. Topics in the social sciences include accounting, computer office systems, criminal justice, economics, education, finance, geography, marketing, legal studies, physical education, political science, psychology, recreation, sociology, social work, special education and tourism. As you can see, this subject area covers many diverse topics that may not seem related in any way. However, there is a single thread of commonality -- they all deal with special phases of human interaction and society.

As was determined in Chapter 6, specialized library reference sources can be placed in the following categories:

Almanacs   Directories
Atlases   Encyclopedias
Bibliographies   Handbooks and Manuals
Biographical Works   Indexes & Abstracts
Dictionaries

Keep in mind that all of the sources listed below will not be found in every academic library. These are some of the more common sources within each subject area. To determine if the library you are using has a copy of any of these sources you would use their online catalog to search by title, author or subject.

Almanacs

The almanac of higher education. (1995). Chicago: The University of Chicago Press.

> The editors of *The Chronicle of Higher Education* offer yearly information about students, faculty, staff and institutions in higher education. Statistics concerning individual states are also given.

Nash, J.R. (1981). *Almanac of world crime.* Garden City, NY: Doubleday.

> Do you need to know information about various aspects of criminology such as assassination, bombs, women criminals, terrorism, serial killers, etc.? This resource provides a good overview of crime throughout the world.

The NEA almanac of higher education. (1995). Washington, DC: National Education Association.

> Although some general information is given, this yearly edition chronicles the accomplishments of the National Education Association (NEA).

THINK ABOUT THIS....

You are looking for a reference work in a specific subject area. You do not know what title, author, or subject heading to search. What do you do? Try a keyword search that contains the information you seek. For example, a simple keyword search of *Dictionary and Psychology* or *Atlas and Economic*, etc.

As you can see, not knowing the specific title, author or subject will not keep you from obtaining the source you need. There are ways to locate what you want with keyword searching.

Older Americans almanac. (1994). Detroit, MI: Gale Research.

> Anyone interested in a comprehensive information source on many aspects of older Americans from colonial times to the present should check this one out. Includes history, finances, relationships, health, employment, lifestyles, law, politics and many more subjects about aging.

Ginsberg, L. *Social work almanac.* (1995). Washington, DC: National Association of Social Workers.

> As stated in its introduction, this is a book which offers information about the predominent current social issues and social programs. Chapters include children, education, demographics, health, mental illness, older adults and much more.

The World Almanac Book of World War II. (1981). New York: World Almanac Publications.

> This includes a chronological study of the period beginning with "The Approach to War (1919)" and concluding with "The Aftermath" (1950). It offers a day-by-day recording of the political and military happenings along with statistical tables, biographies, various subject divisions and an index.

As you can see there is a wide variety of almanacs available for you to use. These are but a few of them, so when in need of an almanac on a specific subject, use the online catalog to determine what your library has to offer. The following is a list of other almanacs that might be of interest to you.

Almanac of American politics.

Almanac of business and industrial financial ratios.

Almanac of China's economy.

Almanac of the federal judiciary.

Louis Rukeyser's business almanac.

Standard education almanac.

Atlases

Boyd, A. (1987). *An atlas of world affairs.* New York: Methuen.

> Maps and explanation text for countries and regions around the world. Also includes chapters on people, power, oil, nuclear geography, minerals, the sea, minorities, etc. Includes index.

> ## CASE IN POINT
>
> In one of your business classes you decide to write a term paper on the effects that the cost of manufacturing airplanes has on the price of airline tickets. You begin your research using the business sources that you have located. But keep in mind that there might be sources in the Sciences -- such as Applied Science and Technology Index -- that would also be of help for your paper.
>
> Also consider the relationship that most of the subjects in the social sciences have with current events. That means currency of information is important. As was learned in a previous chapter, books do not always contain the most current information. Many of the sources listed in Chapter 4 and in this chapter will provide a good broad base of information, but newspaper and journal articles will provide the most recent developments.

Gilbert, M. (1971). *First World War atlas*. New York: Macmillan.

> Offers maps ranging from a prelude to WWI and ending with the war's aftermath. Breakdown by year -- 1914 - 1918 and for war in the air and on the seas. Includes bibliography and index.

Kurian, G. T. (1983). *Atlas of the Third World*. New York: Facts on File.

> This 381 page work gives social, economic and political information for separate countries and for the entire Third World. Has an index, but no bibliography.

These are other atlases that may be of interest:

The atlas of American higher education.

Atlas of economic mineral deposits.

Atlas of the 1990 census.

Atlas of the second world war.

Harper atlas of world history.

A world atlas of military history.

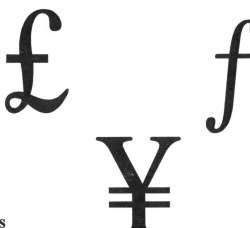

Bibliographies

Baatz, C. A. (1980). *The philosophy of education: A guide to information sources*. Detroit, MI: Gale Research.

> Good bibliography for anyone wanting books or journal articles about the philosophy of education. Entries are annotated and there are subject, author and title indexes.

Conrad, J. H. (1982). *Reference sources in social work: An annotated bibliography*. Metuchen, NJ: Scarecrow Press.

> The bibliography is broken down into broad subjects and subdivisions and has over 600 entries.

> ### THINK ABOUT THIS....
>
> Sometimes the most direct approach to finding reference resources is not always the best. For example, if you were looking for a bibliography on a particular subject the most logical keyword search might be *death penalty and bibliography*. However, the word "bibliography" might not appear in the record and you would get zero hits. A better search strategy could be *death penalty and (guide or sources or literature or bibliograph?)*. The point is to keep trying until you have exhausted the possibilities!

Current contents. (1974-). Philadelphia: Institute for Scientific Information.

> This weekly publication reproduces the tables of contents for over 1,000 books with more than one author. Arranged by subject, title, and author. Contents are grouped into broad subject divisions.

Daniells, L. M. (1985). *Business information sources*. Berkeley: University of California Press.

> Good basic list of information sources on the subjects of investment, insurance, management, statistics, etc.

Durnin, R. G. (1982). *American education: A guide to information sources*. Detroit, MI: Gale Research.

> This is a bibliography of both general and specific books that deal with elementary, secondary and higher education. Provides subject arrangement with an index.

Mark, C. (1976). *Sociology of America: A guide to information sources*. Detroit, MI: Gale Research.

> Do you need a book written in the English language on American life? This is a listing of over 1,800 books from the general to the more specific. Indexes by author, title and subject.

Quay, R. H. (1980). *Index to anthologies on postsecondary education, 1960-1978*. Westport, CT: Greenwood Press.

> It is exactly what the title indicates, an index of anthologies divided into several categories including, history, faculty, students, politics, governance, curriculum & instruction, legal issues, institutional goals, etc.

Wang, A. Y. (1989). *Author's guide to journals in the behavioral sciences*. Hillsdale, NJ: Lawrence Erlbaum Associates.

> As the introduction indicates this book's purpose is to provide information about the editorial policies of journals of interest to behavioral scientists and psychologists.

Other bibliographies that might be of interest include:

Bibliographic guide to educational research.

Bibliography of Canadian law.

Bibliography of mental tests and rating.

Genocide: A critical bibliographic review.

The Harvard list of books in pyschology.

International guide to accounting journals.

The Negro in the United States: A selected bibliography.

The philosopher's guide to sources, research tools, professional life, and related fields.

Sources of information in the social sciences.

Statistics sources: A subject guide to data on industrial, business and other statistics sources.

Women: A bibliography.

Biographical Works

American men and women of science: Social and behavioral sciences. (1971-Present). New York: R.R. Bowker.

Provides brief biographies of more than 100,000 persons in the fields of economics, political science, psychology and sociology.

Directory of American scholars. (1982). New York: R.R. Bowker.

Gives information for persons who are active scholars in the United States and Canada.

Ingham, J.N. (1983). *Biographical dictionary of American business leaders*. Westport, CT: Greenwood Press.

This multi-volume work offers brief biographical information for more than 1,000 business leaders. Breakdown is according to industry, company, birthplace, religion, ethnicity and women.

Zusne, L. (1984). *Biographical dictionary of psychology*. Westport, CT: Greenwood Press.

Over 1,000 brief biographies are offered on prominent psychologists. Particular emphasis was placed on the importance to the area of psychology of the person included.

Who's who among students in American universities & colleges. (1935-Present). Tuscaloosa, AL: Randall Publishing.

Information about students (provided by the students) which is "generally accurate information." Entries include categories of birth, parents, degree, activities and employment.

Women educators in the United States, 1820-1993. (1994). Westport, CT: Greenwood Press.

This work profiles sixty-six women American educators. Biographies are fairly extensive and includes a bibliography, along with works by, and about, the the educator. Each biography begins with a short summary about the person.

Other sources to consult for biographical information are:

Biographical dictionary of American educators.

Leaders in education.

Names in the history of psychology.

Outstanding women athletes.

Who's who in American education.

Who's who in American politics.

Who's who in finance and industry.

Who's who in labor.

THINK ABOUT THIS....

To find information about a person, it is not necessary to begin by locating a biographical source dedicated to a specific subject field. In a previous chapter *BioBase* was discussed. Look up the person's name in *BioBase*. *BioBase* will lead you to general biographical resources plus specialized resources in your person's field.

Dictionaries

Specialized dictionaries are very important in subject-specific research. Many fields contain jargon not understood by the general public. The dictionaries spotlighted below are not "general" works. They have a narrow focus and are listed to show the areas within the social sciences that have titles devoted to them. Keep in mind that these are a selected few of the many that exist.

Black's law dictionary. (1979). St. Paul, MN: West Publishing.

Offers definitions for legal terms and concepts. Includes a guide to pronunciation and a list of abbreviations.

Dictionary of concepts in general psychology. (1988). New York: Greenwood Press.

Good general source for terminology in psychology. Contains an author and subject index.

Dictionary of instructional technology. (1986). New York: Nichols Publishing.

More than 2,800 British and American terms are defined in this work. Sometimes illustrations are given to enhance the concept. See and See Also cross-referencing are provided.

A dictionary of the social sciences. (1964). New York: The Free Press.

Compiled under the direction of The United Nations Educational, Scientific, and Cultural Organization (UNESCO), this is one of many "general" works covering the social sciences.

A modern dictionary of geography. (1986). Baltimore: Edward Arnold.

Targeted for students in secondary education and beginning college courses. This is not an attempt to define the more common terms, but to address unusual and "bizarre" terms.

Monkhouse, F. J. (1970). *A dictionary of geography*. Chicago: Aldine Publishing.

Do you need to know the definition for allogenic, basalt, cuesta, glebe, megalopolis, tidal current or one of hundreds of other terms? Look for it here. It also includes abbreviations and the origin of foreign words.

The pocket economist. (1984). New York: Cambridge University Press.

This is a guide to the jargon used in economics. It is by no means comprehensive. At the end of the entries is a listing of sources for further reading.

The public policy dictionary. (1987). Santa Barbara, CA: ABC-CLIO.

General source that includes terminology for the person not well versed in political science. Terms are defined and then there is offered a paragraph of "Significance." The Significance paragraph discusses the historical and present relevance of the concept.

Shefski, B. (1978). *Running Press glossary of football language*. Philadelphia: Running Press.

> Do you ever wonder what the football players, referees, owners, agents, coaches, etc. are talking about when they use terminology that you are unfamiliar with? This is the source to use to become more proficient in discussing the game.

Statt, D. (1981). *Dictionary of psychology*. New York: Barnes & Noble Books.

> General, non-comprehensive source for those beginning to study in the field of psychology.

A student's dictionary of psychology. (1993). New York: Edward Arnold.

> This is a general guide for students who are studying psychology. Includes information to prominent psychologists and publications that would be of interest to the reader.

Thomsett, M. C. (1989). *Insurance dictionary*. Jefferson, NC: McFarland & Company.

> This work not only offers a glossary of terms, as expected, but gives addresses for state and Canadian companies and a listing of abbreviations.

Vogt, P. W. (1993). *Dictionary of statistics and methodology*. Newbury Park, CA: Sage Publications.

> It alphabetizes letter-by-letter, rather than word-by-word. Focuses more on concepts (correlation coefficient, ramdom sampling, etc.) than calculations. Verbal definitions are given, along with mathematical symbols when necessary.

Some other titles for the social sciences include:

The American political dictionary.

Crime dictionary.

Dictionary of business and economics.

Dictionary of business and management.

Dictionary of education.

Dictionary of medical folklore.

Dictionary of modern sociology.

Dictionary of race and ethnic relations.

Dictionary of reading and learning disability.

Educational administration glossary.

The language of real estate.

Microsoft Press computer dictionary.

The MIT dictionary of modern economics.

Oxford campanion to the mind.

The peace and nuclear war dictionary.

Que's computer user's dictionary.

Statistical vocabulary.

Words for the wise: A field guide to academic terms.

Directories

As noted in a previous chapter, directories offer information about people, organizations, institutions, businesses, and other single or group items. It is a listing of general information about which might include addresses, employment, purposes, goals, dues, officers or administrators, achievements, etc.

Directory of U.S. labor organizations. (1994). Washington, DC: BNA Books.

> Gives addresses, phone numbers, fax numbers, officers, etc. for labor organizations. Also has sections on abbreviations, membership data, union reporting requirements, common name of organizations and structure charts for AFL-CIO.

Education directory: Public school systems. (1969/70-). Washington, DC: National Center for Education Statistics.

> It is arranged by state and provides information about local public school systems; including names of administrators, location, grades, number of students and number (and names) of schools in the system.

Federal statistical directory: The guide to personnel and data sources (28th ed.). (1987). New York: Oryx Press.

> Offers officers, addresses and phone numbers for the Executive Branch of the federal government. Also includes some state agencies.

Directory of corporate affiliations. (1995). New Providence, NJ: National Register Publishing.

> This six-volume work includes listings for public and private companies, with some international ones also profiled. The "Master Index" allows the user to locate the company they wish, as many companies are subsidiaries of larger ones. Information includes employment, sales, type of business and percentage of ownership by the parent compnay.

International directory of social science organizations. (1981-). Stockholm: Almqvist & Wiksell.

> As the title implies this is a source of information about social science organizations around the world.

Kruzas, A. T. (1982). *Social service organizations and agencies directory.* Detroit, MI: Gale Research.

> Divided into subject chapters and further sub-divided according to type of organization. Indexed by name and keyword.

The mental health yearbook/directory. (1979/80-). New York: Van Nostrand Reinhold.

> Combination directory and yearbook for programs, publications, services, facilities for mental health.

National faculty directory. (1970-Present). New York: Gale Research.

> This is an alphabetical list of teaching faculties at junior colleges, 4-year colleges and universities in the United States and selected schools in Canada. It includes addresses for the faculty members and telephone numbers for the individual institutions.

Regional directory of minority & women-owned business firms. (1988). Lombard, IL: Business Research Services.

> This "South Central" edition is divided by SIC codes. Includes name of business, location, telephone number, minority type, etc. Also has cross-reference by name of firm.

Sorkins' directory of business & government. (1995). Chesterfield, MO: Sorkins' Directories.

> Each multi-volume directory focuses on a metropolitan area. Alphabetical listing of brief company profiles for businesses and government agencies.

State administrative officials classified by function. (1995). Lexington, KY: The Council of State Governments.

> As the title states, this is a listing of state administrative officials, divided by office and/or subject -- adjutant general, chief justice, corrections, ethics, health, lottery, state police, veterinarian, etc. Offers address, phone and fax numbers.

Ward's business directory of U.S. private and public companies. (1996). New York: Gale Research.

> This is a comprehensive guide to more than 130,000 companies. Arranged by company name, geographic location and type of industry. Offers ranking by sales and industry activity within each state.

World directory of social science institutions. (1982). Paris: UNESCO.

> Gives information for more than 2,000 national and international organizations. Arranged by country and offers indexing by subject and name.

The above sources are only a few of those that exist for the social sciences. Use the online catalog to locate others of interest. Below are a few more sample titles.

American Bar Association directory.

Association of American Geographers directory.

Business organizations and agencies directory.

Directory of U.S. military bases worldwide.

Guide to American graduate schools.

Hoover's handbook of American business.

Hoover's handbook of world business.

The international directory of recreation.

The Missouri legal directory.

The national civil rights directory.

National directory of law enforcement.

NLN guide to undergraduate RN education.

Peterson's guide to graduate programs.

Statistical services directory.

CASE IN POINT

A student is asked to prepare a list and find information for the school districts in a specific county in Missouri. The student could find a telephone book for the county and make a list of each school district, then call each one to get the information relevant to completing the assignment -- Or the student could go to the Government Documents area of the library to see if the state produces a directory of school districts that would give that information.

Encyclopedias

As noted earlier, if you are unsure what a particular subject is about it might be wise to find a brief summary of it and read it first before doing extensive research. Getting an overview of a subject is helpful to know if a research report can be completed on the entire subject, or only on a portion of it.

The encyclopedia of aging. (1995). New York: Springer Publishing.

> A one-volume source developed with the help of more than 200 contributors, this work offers several hundred terms and concepts for the field of gerontology. The second edition provides more emphasis on health and geriatrics.

Encyclopedia of banking and finance. (1983). Boston: Bankers Publishing.

> Available since 1924, this one-volume work provides more than 4,000 entries for basic business, banking and finance. Quick index in the back.

Encyclopedia of careers and vocational guidance. (1990). Chicago: J.G. Ferguson Publishing.

> This four-volume set has a general information section, a description of industries, a description of specific jobs, with regard to educational requirements and necessary training. Index is included for each volume.

Encyclopedia of education. (1971). New York: Macmillan and Company.

> Ten volumes with more than 1,000 entries about various aspects of education, with emphasis on American education. Includes index.

Encyclopedia of occultism & parapsychology. (1984). Detroit, MI: Gale Research.

> Consists of three volumes. Gives thousands of entries. Volume 3 includes a general index, a topical index, listing of periodicals, listing of plants and flowers, and a list of societies and organizations.

Encyclopedia of physical education, fitness, and sports. (1981). Salt Lake City: Brighton Publishing.

> Multi-volume work provides thousands of entries on the various topics of physical education, fitness, health, programs, professions, organizations and sports.

Encyclopedia of social work. (1995). Washington, DC: National Association of Social Workers.

> Three-volume set deals with both practice and research of social work. Offers 290 entries, and 142 biographies. Each volume is indexed.

Encyclopedia of world crime. (1990). Wilmette, IL: CrimeBooks.

> As the introduction states, it aims to "present the complete historical perspective of crime, from ancient times to the present." Four volumes. Also includes key to abbreviations and index.

Encyclopedia of world cultures. (1991). Boston, MA: G.K. Hall and Company.

> Multi-volume set, with each volume containing cultural summaries, maps, filmography, ethnonym index of alternate cultural names, and a glossary of scientific and technical terms.

International encyclopedia of the social sciences. (1968). New York: Macmillan.

> Topical and biographical articles are offered in this eighteen-volume set. A bibliography is given at the end of each article.

Below are other encyclopedias that may be of interest.

The Baseball Encyclopedia.

Cyclopedia of American government.

Encyclopedia of advertising.

Encyclopedia of black America.

Encyclopedia of criminology.

Encyclopedia of economics.

The encyclopedia of management.

Encyclopedia of sociology.

Encyclopedia of superstitions, folklore, and the occult sciences of the world.

Encyclopedia of the third world.

The international encyclopedia of higher education.

International encyclopedia of population.

International encyclopedia of statistics.

Teacher's encyclopedia.

Gazetteers

In Chapter 4 you were introduced to a couple of general gazetteers. Since you already know that a gazetteer is a place-name directory listing places and offering information about them, it is not necessary to give explanations for the sources below. Instead, a list is provided so you will know a few of the titles that do exist.

Aboriginal place names and their meanings.

The American counties.

Bartholomew gazetteer of Britain.

The cities and towns of China: A geographical dictionary.

Concise Oxford dictionary of English place names.

Dictionary of altitudes in the Dominion of Canada.

Dictionary of Greek and Roman geography.

Gazetteer of China.

A gazetteer of Greece.

Gazetteer of India.

Handbook of geographical nicknames.

Historical and political gazetteer of Afghanistan.

Historical gazetteer of Iran.

Johnston's Gazetteer of Scotland, including a glossary of the most common Gaelic names.

Place-name changes since 1900: A world gazetteer.

Pronouncing gazetteer and geographical dictionary of the Philippine Islands.

Provinces and provincial capitals of the world.

South African place-names, past and present.

Topographical dictionary of Ireland.

Handbooks and Manuals

Accountant's handbook of formulas and tables. (1988). Englewood Cliffs, NJ: Prentice Hall.

    Information to aid in programming computer applications and in checking and verifying computer printouts of tough math problems. Not for the novice.

The complete handbook for the entrepreneur. (1990). Englewood Cliffs, NJ: Prentice Hall.

    This book is intended for those who are not afraid to seek opportunities where others are. Gives practical information and examples for success. Addresses all aspects in starting your business.

The handbook of practical psychology. (1980). Englewood Cliffs, NJ: Prentice Hall.

    This is a reference book of topics concerning psychology. It is geared for the person who has not had a chance to study psychology. Very general in nature. Subject index in the back.

Handbook of world education. (1992). Houston, TX: American Collegiate Service.

    This guide compares higher education and educational systems around the world. Arranged alphabetically by name of country. Each chapter is divided into background, elementary and secondary education, higher education and current trends.

How to prepare for the GMAT. (1993). New York: Harcourt Brace Jovanovich.

    Begins by giving a description of what the General Management Admission Test (GMAT) is and how it is scored. It then offers tips and strategies for taking the GMAT, along with sample questions and the answer key.

Publication manual of the American Psychological Association (4th ed.). (1994). Washington, DC: The Association.

    This style manual prepares the writer to organize the research paper, thesis, dissertation, etc., into the form and style accepted by readers in the field of psychology. Offers form and style for grammar, punctuation, notes, bibliography, title page, etc.

CASE IN POINT

    You are asked to write a five-page paper about heredity and criminal behavior. Rather than locate the myriad of articles and books that might exist about this subject you would be wise to find an encyclopedic work about crime or criminal justice to see what this subject is all about. After reading the article in the encyclopedia you might decide that you could construct a five page paper on the "Juke Myth" rather than try to cover the entire topic in five pages.

Reference manual for office workers. (1977). Beverly Hills, CA: Glencoe Press.

> Need a ready reference for correct grammar, punctuation, capitalization, spelling, abbreviations, business reports, filing systems, units of measure, numbers and symbols, and other office procedures? Look no further; you have found it. Recent versions address computer aspects.

The special education handbook. (1991). Philadelphia: Open University Press.

> Basic reference source for those in special education. Contains terms, topics, biographies, issues and information about societies and associations.

Statistical handbook on aging Americans. (1994). Phoenix, AZ: Oryx Press.

> Contains a glossary, list of sources and index. Breaks information into the broad subject divisions of demographics, social characteristics, health, employment, economic conditions, and expenditures.

The thesis writer's handbook. (1987). West Linn, OR: Alcove Publishing.

> Offers examples and instructions on writing using Chicago, MLA APA style manuals. This edition is dated, but there are others more current that will guide you through the correct procedures for writing that term paper or thesis.

There are probably more handbooks and manuals in your library's reference collection than any other type of source. Below are listed a few of them. Many are not your ordinary handbook or manual and the list is intended to get you to think of the various possibilities.

Bankers desk reference.

Consumer protection manual.

Famous first facts about Negroes.

A guide to writing and publishing in the social and behavioral sciences.

Handbook of adult education.

Handbook of advertising management.

The handbook of international direct marketing.

Handbook of North American Indians.

Handbook of research design and social measurement.

How to get government grants.

Lawyer's desk book.

Narcotics and drug abuse, A to Z.

The psychotherapy handbook.

Public relations handbook.

Indexes and Abstracts

The tools listed in this section are important for completing papers and class projects. Indexing and abstracting tools give citations, and sometimes full-text articles, to magazines, journals, research reports, book chapters and newspapers. Some indexes are printed in annual book format. Others are available on computers, either online or on CD-ROM. These indexes contain plenty of information to complete most projects.

The indexes and abstracts below are listed alphabetically with no regard for subject matter or format of the index, whether paper or electronic. Many students think that they can use a CD-ROM to locate anything they need. This is not true! Sometimes the information a student needs can only be found in paper format, or perhaps the library does not own the electronic equivalent. Electronic databases are not the *only* research tool to use, or even the *best* tool to use. This listing is not comprehensive. Therefore consult with a library staff member to determine what indexes and abstracts are best for a subject.

ABI/INFORM (1987-Present) [CD-ROM]. Ann Arbor, MI: UMI.

> This is the oldest and largest CD-ROM source of information worldwide for business subjects. It provides citations and summaries to articles about companies and products, trends and conditions of business, corporate strategies and tactics, management policies and techniques, and other topics of interest in the business world. ABI/INFORM indexes and provides abstracts to more than 800 business and trade journals.

Accounting & tax index (1992-Present). Ann Arbor, MI: UMI. (formerly *Accountant's index* (1972-1991).

> It is published quarterly by UMI and is based on the former title which was produced by the American Institute of Certified Public Accountants (AICPA). Indexes over 1,000 journals and deals with information concerning accounting and taxation.

Business periodicals index (1958-Present). New York: H. W. Wilson.

> This is the most general of business indexes. Published monthly (except August), this index covers over 150 English business periodicals, including *The Wall Street Journal*. Book reviews are included in the back. Articles about a particular company are listed by that company's name.

Compact Disclosure [CD-ROM]. (1986-). Ann Arbor, MI: UMI.

> This database provides current financial and management information on more than 12,000 publicly held companies. The data is taken from reports filed with the U.S. Securities and Exchange Commission (SEC). Companies included in the database sell goods and/or services to the public have at least 500 shareholders of 1 class of stock and at least $5 million in assets. It is updated bi-monthly.

Criminal justice abstracts. (1977-Present). New York: Willow Tree Press. (Formerly *Crime and Delinquency Literature* 1970-1976).

> Indexes journals, reports and current books worldwide. This publication is closely related to the Criminal Justice/ NCCD Collection at Rutgers University.

Criminal justice periodical index. (1975-Present). Ann Arbor, MI: UMI.

> Provides indexing for more than 100 U.S. and Canadian journals in the areas of corrections, criminal law, criminology, drug abuse, family law, juvenile justice, police studies, prison administration, rehabilitation and security systems. It is published every four months with a year-end cumulation.

Current index to journals in education - CIJE. (1969-Present). Phoenix, AZ: Oryx Press.

> This index has comprehensive coverage of almost 800 education periodicals, dealing with all aspects of education. The subject/author index refers the user to an annotation section arranged by entry numbers. *CIJE* is part of the electronic database *ERIC*, which will be discussed later.

Dissertation Abstracts Ondisc [CD-ROM]. (1861-Present). Ann Arbor, MI: UMI.

> Dissertation Abstracts contains bibliographic citations and abstracts for doctoral dissertations as well as some master's theses completed at accredited North American colleges and universities since 1861. The user can search for specific words or phrases by specific field or anywhere that they may appear in the reference or abstract. It is updated quarterly.

Educational administration abstracts. (1966-Present). Thousand Oaks, CA: Corwin Press.

> It is published four times per year, covering books, journals and other kinds of materials. Subject areas include anything concerning school administration. It indexes articles by author and subject.

Education index. (1929-Present). Thousand Oaks, CA: Corwin Press.

> This work provides subject and author indexing to English language education publications -- books, pamphlets, periodicals and yearbooks. It is published monthly, except July and August, with annual cumulations.

ERIC - Educational Resources Information Center [CD-ROM]. (1966-Present). Norwood, MA: SilverPlatter International.

> ERIC is an information service administered by the U.S. Department of Education. Its mission is selecting, acquiring, indexing, storing, retrieving and disseminating education-related materials. ERIC interprets "education" very broadly, and therefore might be of use to a researcher no matter what the subject. This CD-ROM database is the electronic equivalent of two paper indexes - *Current Index to Journals in Education* (CIJE) for periodical articles and *Resources in Education* (RIE) for research reports on microfiche. The companion volume, *Thesaurus of ERIC Descriptors*, helps the researcher select subject headings and search terms.

Exceptional child education resources. (1977-Present). Reston, VA: Council for Exceptional Children. (formerly *Exceptional child education abstracts* 1969-1977).

> Published quarterly by The Council for Exceptional Children. Indexed by author, title and subject. Entries lead to the entry/abstract section. Coverage includes *ERIC* documents, journals, books, dissertations and nonprint materials.

Geographical abstracts: Human geography. (1989-Present). New York: Elsevier.

> Provides comprehensive coverage of the human geography subject areas -- economic, environmental, population, historical, rural and urban studies, agriculture, industry and services, and many more. Subject and regional indexes lead user to entry section. Annual geographical, subject and author index. Prior to 1989 it was *Geo Abstracts*.

Geographical abstracts: Physical geography. (1989-Present). New York: Elsevier.

> This provides a comprehensive look at the physical geography subject areas -- sedimentology, landforms, hydrology, meteorology, climatology, remote sensing, photogrammetry and cartography. Regional index leads user to entry section. The annual cumulation contains a subject, country, and author section. Prior to 1989 it was *Geo Abstracts*.

Higher education abstracts. (1964-Present). Claremont, CA: Claremont Graduate School.

> Indexes information about students, faculty and administrators in higher education. Issued quarterly by the Claremont Graduate School. Author and subject index directs user to the abstract/entry section.

Index to legal periodicals. (1908-Present). New York: H.W. Wilson.

> Published monthly, except September, by the H.W. Wilson Company. It indexes legal periodicals from the United States, Great Britain, Canada, Ireland, Australia, and New Zealand. Materials are from journals, biographies, book reviews, commentaries and case notes. There is both a subject and an author index and a table of cases.

Library literature. (1921-present). New York: H. W. Wilson.

> Since 1984 it is available in electronic format. This index covers library and information sciences, indexing approximately 200 international library periodicals, plus books, theses, papers, and films. It is a good resource for finding articles about using information technology, such as the Internet. Updated quarterly.

National criminal justice reference service - NCJRS [CD-ROM]. (1972-Present). Washington, DC: U.S. Department of Justice, National Institute of Justice.

The National Institute of Justice (NIJ) is the U.S. Department of Justice's research and development agency. NIJ created *NCJRS* as a clearinghouse for criminal justice information. The database contains over 120,000 citations to journals, books, government reports, congressional hearings, audiovisuals, conference presentations and more.

Physical education index. (1978-Present). Cape Girardeau, MO: BenOak Publishing.

This index has citations to English-language domestic and foreign journals. Covers the subjects of dance, health, physical education, physical therapy, recreation, sports and sports medicine. Published quarterly, with an annual cumulation.

Physical fitness/sports medicine. (1978-Present). Washington, DC: President's Council on Physical Fitness and Sports.

Published quarterly by the President's Council on Physical Fitness and Sports. The subjects indexed include exercise physiology, sports injuries, physical conditioning and the medical aspects of exercise from over 3,000 English-language foreign and domestic journals.

PsycLIT [CD-ROM]. (1974-Present). Norwood, MA: SilverPlatter International.

PsycLIT is the electronic equivalent to *Psychological Abstracts*, which began publication in 1927. It covers over 1,300 journals, some in foreign languages. The American Psychological Association incorporates publications from related disciplines, such as sociology, linguistics, medicine, law, physiology, business, psychiatry and anthropology.

Public affairs international. (1991-present). New York: Public Affairs Information Service. (Formerly *Public affairs information service bulletin* (*PAIS Bulletin*). (1915-1990). New York: Public Affairs Information Service.

PAIS indexes periodicals, books, government publications, and the reports of public and private organizations pertaining to the subjects of economics, political science, public administration, international law and relations,demography, business, education, finance, social work, and other related fields. It indexes by subject and by some authors and titles. This is a great place to find materials that aren't indexed anywhere else.

Resources in education - RIE. (1966-Present). Phoenix, AZ: Oryx Press.

This index is included in ERIC (see above). This is an index to the ERIC research reports. It is cumulated annually. *RIE* has two main sections: the document entry (resume) section and the index section. Index section is by author, subject and institution, and it guides the user to the entry section where pertinent information about the research report can be found. The entry (resume) section is arranged by the "ED Number" of the entry. This number also serves as the call number for the microfiche item.

CASE IN POINT

You have chosen the subject of social behavior of college students as a major research project. You have decided to look in ERIC for articles and research reports. You find several items that are useful and decide to quit researching and start writing the 20-page paper. Have you exhausted the possibilities? Nope! You have merely scratched the surface. Other sources you could use are *Education Index, PsycLit,* or *Sociofile.* It is possible that ERIC contains more than enough information to complete the assignment, but you need to think ahead and be prepared to go beyond your first choice.

> ## THINK ABOUT THIS....
>
> In today's world of academe, college professors are striving to get promoted to assistant, associate, or full-professor. You have probably heard of the phrase "publish or perish." This refers to the fact that promotion at colleges and universitites relies heavily on a person's publishing track record. To take that one step further, many universities are also looking at who is citing a person's publication. If it is being cited, then it is being read, and it is also offering content for others to use in their publication. *Social Science Citation Index* is the source to use.

Social sciences index [CD-ROM]. (1984-Present). New York: H. W. Wilson.

> This index was formerly *International Index*, 1907-1965; *Social Sciences and Humanities Index*, 1965-1974; and *Social Sciences Index*, 1975-1983. It includes articles from English language periodicals in the fields of anthropology, economics, geography, environmental sciences, criminology, law, political science, sociology, psychology and other related subjects. The paper index is published quarterly and gives a listing of book reviews in the back.

Social sciences citation index. (1972-Present). Philadelphia: Institute for Scientific Information.

> Need to find out who is citing an article that you wrote, or do you have one good article about a particular subject and want to see who is citing it in their "related" article? This resource can do that! Issued three time per year and covers more than 2,000 journals.

Social work abstracts plus [CD-ROM]. (1977-Present). Norwood, MA: SilverPlatter International.

> This CD-ROM contains two databases produced by the National Association of Social Workers. The first database, *Social Work Abstracts*, contains more than 26,000 citations of articles from social work and related journals. It is an exact reproduction of the paper *Social Work Research and Abstracts*. The second database, *The Register of Clinical Social Workers* gives the address, phone number, educational background and specialization for clinical social workers.

Sociofile [CD-ROM]. (1974-Present). Norwood, MA: SilverPlatter International.

> This product is a subset of *Sociological Abstracts*. It covers sociology and related disciplines with bibliographic citations and abstracts from more than 1,600 journals in 30 different languages from more than 50 countries. It is updated twice a year. It also includes relevant dissertations taken from *Dissertation Abstracts International*.

Internet Sources

As stated in chapter 8, the Internet is growing and developing very quickly. There are thousands of sites that have information that might be useful to someone doing research in the social sciences. The information you will find is usually not the same kinds of things found in a library, like magazine articles and books, but there are other resources that can be useful to students. Yahoo and other search engines were discussed to show you how to find information. With the number of new sites appearing each week, it is a good idea to not limit yourself to those sites that you have already visited. Below are a few of the many sites which can be found on the Internet. Keep in mind that these sites were available when research was completed on this book but could have changed locations or disappeared. When the name is not sufficient to identify the site, then a brief explanation is offered of what it contains.

Internet Resources

Accounting Department Management & Administration Report (Journal) [Online]. Available: *http://ioma.com/ioma/admar/*

U.S. Colleges and Universities Listing [Online]. Available: *http://www.yahoo.com/Regional/Countries/United_States/Education/Colleges_and_Universities/all.html*

Americans with Disabilities Act (ADA) [Online]. Available: *gopher://wiretap.spies.com/ 00/Gov/disable.act*

Bureau of Justice Statistics (Crime) [Online]. Available: *http://www.ch.search.org/*

Budget of the United States [Online]. Available: *http://www.doc.gov/inquery/Budget-FY97/index.html*

Census Statistics(1990) [Online]. Available: *http://www.oseda.missouri.edu/usinfo.html*

Criminal Justice Links [Online]. Available: *http://www.ncjrs.org/*

Demography & Population Studies Register [Online]. Available: *http:// coombs.anu.edu.au/ResFacilities/DemographyPage.html*

Economics Server [Online]. Available: *gopher://econ.lsa.umich.edu/*

Electronic Journal of Behavior Analysis and Therapy [Online]. Available: *http:// sage.und.nodak.edu/org/jBAT/jbatinfo.html*

Electronic Journal of Sociology [Online]. Available: *http:// olympus.lang.arts.ualberta.ca:8010/*

FindLaw: Supreme Court Opinions [Online]. Available: *http://www.findlaw.com/ casecode/supreme.html*

Guides to Law Resources on the Internet [Online]. Available: *gopher://marvel.loc.gov/11/ global/law/guides*

Journal of Finance [Online]. Available: *http://www.cob.ohio-state.edu/dept/fin/journal/ jof.htm*

K12 Net [Online]. Available: *http://www.ggw.org/freenet/k/k12Net/intro to.html*

Managing Credit. Receivables & Collections (Journal) [Online]. Available: *http:// ioma.com/ioma/mcrc/*

Newbie's Guide to Sports [Online]. Available: *http://ug.cs.dal.ca:3400/sports.html*

Population Studies Center (University of Pennsylvania) [Online]. Available: *gopher:// lexis.pop.upenn.edu*

Internet Resources

Psych Page [Online]. Available: *http://www.jetlink.net/~blueone/psych.html*
  Links to professional organizations, journals, and other resources.

Social Work Action Network [Online]. Available: *http://www.sc.edu/swan/*

The universal currency converter™ [Online]. Available: http://www.xe.net/currency/
  Convert any amount between any of 69 forms of monetary exchange. The rates of exchange are taken from data prepared by the Bank of Montreal's Treasury Group for Canada's national newspaper, The Globe and Mail.

U.S. Federal and State Government Sites [Online]. Available: *http://www.obscure.org/~jaws/government.html*

The U.S. House of Representatives internet law library presidential documents [Online]. Available: http://law.house.gov/13.htm

White House frequently asked questions [Online]. Available: *ftp://ftp.sura.net*

World constitutions [Online]. Available: *gopher://wiretap.spies.com:70/11/Gov/World*
  This site contains 26 constitutions from the Magna Charta to the 1992 Chinese Declaration of Human Rights

World Wide Web Virtual Library-Asian Studies [Online]. Available: *http://coombs.anu.edu.au/WWWVL*-AsianStudies.html

World Wide Web Virtual Library-Education [Online]. Available: *http://info.cern.ch/hypertext/DataSources/bySubject/*Education/Overview.html

Yahoo resources in political science [Online]. Available: *http://www.yahoo.com/Social Science/Political Science/Indices*

EXERCISE 1

Name _____ Section _____

Locate the following books on the bookshelves using the title and author given. On this page:

  1. Write down the call number of the book.

  2. Locate the page and write down the first three words on that page.

  3. IF THE BOOK IS NOT ON THE SHELF, give the call numbers of the book which come immediately before and after the space where the book should be.

PLEASE RETURN ALL BOOKS TO THEIR PROPER PLACE ON THE SHELF

<u>Call No.</u>   <u>First three words from page indicated</u>

Unionizing the armed forces, Krendel & Samoff, p. 54.

1. _____   _____

Case closed, Gerald L. Posner, p. 194.

2. _____   _____

The transplant, A. Q. Mowbray, p. 92.

3. _____   _____

Theatre of crisis, Diana Taylor, p. 4.

4. _____   _____

Cheetahs of the Serengeti plains, T. M. Caro, p. 137.

5. _____   _____

African pygmies, Luigi Luca Cavalli-Sforza, p. 17.

6. _____   _____

The way the world works, Jude Wanniski, p. 213.

7. _____   _____

Ku kanaka stand tall, George Huen Starford Kanahele, p. 263

8. _____   _____

Last stand at Rosebud creek, Michael Parfit, p. 63.

9. _____   _____

On the brink, Blight and Welch, p. 221.

10. _____   _____

Jimmy Carter, Mazlish and Diamond, p. 46.

11. _____   _____

Big Daddy from the pedernales, Paul K. Conkin, p. 82.

12. _____   _____

Take my word for it, Vernon Pizer, p. 56.

13. _____   _____

The quest for the holy grail, Fred. W. Locke, p. 63.

14. _____   _____

The age of hair, Barbara Lee Horn, p. 79.

15. _____   _____

Ethnicity & assimilation, Robert M. Jiobu, p. 132.

16. _____   _____

You, my brother, Philip Burton, p. 156.

17. _____   _____

The agenda, Bob Woodward, p. 133.

18. _____   _____

Of mice and women, Bjorkqvist and Niemela, p. 38.

19. _____   _____

The moral collapse of the university, Wilshire, p. 69.

20. _____   _____

EXERCISE 2

Name _____ Section _____

I. Locate answers to the following questions using <u>general encyclopedias</u>. Be sure to note the answer to the question *and* where the information was found.

Example:	**What is the name of the fruit called monkey bread?** *Baobab, <u>World Book</u>, Vol. 2, p. 70.*

1. Who was the first vice president of the United States?

2. What is the complete name of the Mormon Church?

3. What state is known as the Hoosier State?

4. Who were the members of the Apollo 11 flight crew?

5. What is the major food source for a Koala Bear?

II. Locate answers to the following questions using the ready reference sources noted. Give the answer, name of source (if source is not given specifically) and page number.

1. What is the population of Worth County, Missouri? [Use any general almanac]

2. What state passed the first ordinance of secession? [*Famous First Facts*]

3. How many members does the National Black McDonald's Operators Association have?
   [*Encyclopedia of Associations*]

4. What company makes Halotestin tablets? [*Physician's Desk Reference*]

5. Who is the Lord High Admiral of the United Kingdom? [*Whitaker's Almanack*]

III. Locate answers, and give volume and page numbers, to the following questions, using the biographical source noted.

1. From what college did Eddie Mayes Elliott receive an A.B. degree? [*Who's Who in America*]

2. What is the pseudonym used by Ehrich Weiss? [*Dictionary of American Biography*]

3. Where was George Bernard Shaw born? [*Twentieth Century Authors*]

4. What was Ed Bradley's major at Cheyney State College? [*Current Biography*]

5. What is the birthplace of Ralph Waite? [*Who's Who in America*]

IV. Locate answers to the following questions using geographical sources. Give the answer, citation for the source used, and page number.

1. What famous American once owned the natural bridge over Cedar Creek in Virginia?
        [*Columbia Lippincott Gazetteer of the World*]

2. How many air force bases are located in Colorado?
        [*Rand McNally Commercial Atlas and Marketing Guide* - hint: study the table of contents]

3. In what country is the town of San Francisco de la Caleta located? [*Times Atlas of the World*]

4. In what states are there cities named Warrensburg? [*Columbia Lippincott Gazetteer of the World*]

5. What is the 11th largest Basic Trading Area in the U.S.?
        [*Rand McNally Commercial Atlas and Marketing Guide* - hint: study the table of contents]

EXERCISE 3

Name _____ Section _____

Using the newspaper indexes indicated, locate the citation for the article.
1. **Write down the complete citation.**
2. **Locate the article and write down the title.**

1. *1993 New York Times Index, Volume II.*
Locate an article about the burial of Hugh Rodham.

2. *1992 St. Louis Post Dispatch Index.*
Locate an article about Kurt Vonnegut as a speaker at Washington University.

3. *1990 Wall Street Journal Index, Volume I.*
Locate an article about three types of collision-damage waivers offered by Alamo Rent A Car, Inc.

4. 1995 *Newsbank.*
Locate an article about gambling riverboat legislation in Missouri

5. *NewsBank NewsFile* [CD-ROM]
Locate an article about gang activities at soccer games in England.

6. *1992 Wall Street Journal Index, Volume II.*
Locate an article about William H. Webster being elected as a director of Pinkerton's Inc.

7. April 1865 *New York Times Index*
Locate the first front page article about the assassination of President Lincoln.

8. *1990 St. Louis Post Dispatch Index.*
Locate an article about Senator Roger Wilson calling for Missouri agencies to reduce expenses.

9. 1995 *Newsbank*
Locate a performance review of the band R.E.M.

10. *NewsBank NewsFile* [CD-ROM]
Locate an article with both "Carnival" and "New Orleans" in the headline.

EXERCISE 4

Name _____ Section _____

Periodical indexing is available in print and electronic formats. Locate the correct bibliographic entry of the source given. Write down the citation of the article and answer the question for each of the following:

1. *Poole's Index to Periodical Literature*, Vol. V, 1897-1902.
Locate an article titled "Mozart and his Manuscripts."

Who is the author of the article? _____

2. *Readers' Guide to Periodical Literature*, Vol. 50, 1990.
Locate an article on politics and government in Jordan.

What is the title of the article? _____

3. *ProQuest Periodical Abstracts*, 1994-Present.
Locate an article about Governor Carnahan's pardon of Johnny Lee Wilson in *US News and World Report*.

Who is the author of the article? _____

4. *ProQuest Periodical Abstracts*, 1994-present.
Locate an article about Bjork performing at the Tibetan Freedom Concert.

What is the date of the article? _____

5. *ProQuest Periodical Abstracts*, 1994-Present.
Locate an article about no gambling allowed on the Branson Belle.

What is the name of the journal? _____

6. *Readers' Guide to Periodical Literature*, Vol. 52, 1992.
Locate an article about John F. Kennedy, Jr.

What is the name of the journal? _____

7. *ProQuest Periodical Abstracts*, 1994-Present.
Locate an article about tourism in San Antonio, Texas titled "The pleasures of San Antonio in spring."

What is the date of the article? _____

8. *Poole's Index to Periodical Literature*, Vol. V, 1897-1902.
Locate a poem by A. Fields titled "Round the Far Rocks."

What is the name of the journal? _____

9. *ProQuest Periodical Abstracts*, 1994-Present.
Locate an article about Roger Clinton in Playboy.

What is the date of the article? _____

10. *Readers' Guide to Periodical Literature*, Vol. 53, 1993.
Locate an article about Joe Montana in Newsweek.

What is the title of the article? _____

EXERCISE 5

Name _____ Section _____

Using the author, title, subject heading or call number information given find the information requested in the online catalog. (Disregard the birth and death dates for authors.) When more than one item is found, answer the question using the first entry. Hint: titles are underlined, subject headings are in capital letters.

1. CB5 W5 1968

   title:
   subject heading:

2. Root, Franklin R.

   call number:
   title:

3. LB1044.5 W477

   title:
   publisher:

4. COLOR PHOTOGRAPHY

   title:
   place of publication:

5. Total home security

   call number:
   publisher:

6. I'm from Missouri

   call number:
   number of pages:

7. Northouse, Peter Guy

   call number:
   place of publication:

8. Teams in informative systems development

   call number:
   number of pages:

9. POLICE HORSES

   author:
   height:

10. SUCCESS--CASE STUDIES

    author:
    number of pages:

11.   Memory, David M.

    call number:
    title:

12.   DRUGS--TOXICOLOGY

    author:
    number of pages:

13.   Wright, Milburn D.

    call number:
    title:

14.   LB1043 C48

    author:
    subject heading:

15.   The vibration syndrome

    call number:
    publisher:

16.   BF371 R3

    author:
    subject heading:

17.   A short history of geomorphology

    call number:
    place of publication:

18.   HV8324 .I79 1985

    author:
    publisher:

19.   CUBA--SOCIAL CONDITIONS

    author:
    place of publication:

20.   Neese, William A.

    call number:
    subject heading:

EXERCISE 6

Name _____ Section _____

Directions: Place each row in call number order by putting numbers 1 - 5 over each call number.

PS	PR	PR	PQ	PR
559	5219	132	3939	5219
.R87R8	.R26Q3	T8	.D37E4	R26L5

TD	TD	TD	TD	TD
525	194	624	195	525
.L6S4	.5	.L8A53	.P4U555	.L3J48
	.E58		1978	

KFL	KFL	KFL	KFL	KFL
112	45	45	211	30
.A2	.1	.A212	Z9L68	N48A3
1950	.W35			1910

HT	HT	HT	HT	HT
393	393	393	393	393
.L616	L62R323	.L62L52	.L62R52	L6R52

EXERCISE 7

Final Project
APA References--100 Points

Choose a topic and compile a list of ten bibliographic citations (DO NOT WRITE A PAPER!). To find your ten items, use four kinds of indexes--online catalog, paper index, CD-ROM index and the Internet. Arrange the references in APA style format. After each entry, explain in brackets [ ] how you located each item. The bibliography must be typed or computer generated. Include a cover page.

Sample Bibliography:

EATING DISORDERS AMONG TEENAGERS
REFERENCES

Academy of Science. (1995). <u>Science of eating right.</u> Kansas City, MO: Mid-
    Continent Press.
    [Found in the online catalog searching "s=eating disorders--teenagers"]

Adams, W. E. & de Bruyn, J. (1986). <u>Eating problems for girls and boys</u>.
    New York: International Universities Press.
    [Found in the online catalog searching "K=eating and children"]

American Academy of Child and Adolescent Psychiatry. (1996). Teenagers
    with Eating Disorders [Online]. Available: http://www.cmhc.com/
    factsfam/eating.htm
    [Found in Alta Vista searching "adolescent and anorexia"]

Anorexic students unite for help. (1995, December 22). <u>Redbook, 24,</u> 26.
    [Found in <u>Readers' Guide to Periodical Literature</u> (1995) under "bulimia"]

<u>Children's learning systems.</u> (1994). New York: Academic Press.
    [Found in the online catalog searching "s=eating disorders"]

Dandy, D. D. (1995). Eating your way to trouble [Online]. Available Tel-
    net://amber.nv.umn.edu Directory: pub/etext/1995 File: Anorexia
    [Found in Yahoo using "anorexia" as a search term]

Fouchard, K. (1993). Do eating similarities exist among races and nation-
    alities? <u>Intelligence, 7,</u> 325-356.
    [Found in Life Sciences Index (CD-ROM) searching "eating disorders and
    teenagers"]

Luce, L. (1994). Eating right always (Report No. NCRTO-EE-94-2). Lansing,
    MI: Nutrition Center. (ERIC Document Reproduction Service No. ED 388 993)
    [Found in ERIC [CD-ROM] "eating-disorders and children-"]

Wellman, J., Ambs, A., & Jerue, R. (1995, April 12). Is your eating kill-
    ing you? <u>Science, 46,</u> 44.
    [Found in <u>Humanities Index</u> (1995) using "eating-disorders--kids" as a subject]

Zane, T. Z. (1992). <u>Why eat wrong?</u> Los Angeles: California Press.
    [Found in the online catalog searching "s=eating disorders"]

Glossary of Terms

Abridged Dictionary -- A dictionary that contains fewer than 250,000 terms.

Abstract -- A summary of a book, article or document.

Acronym -- A word or group of letters that is made up of letters of words. An example would be SCUBA (Self-Contained Underwater Breathing Apparatus).

Almanac -- A quick-reference source for looking up information and/or statistics about people, places, and things. An almanac can be general or it can be limited to a specific subject.

Annotation -- A summary describing a particular piece of material.

Atlas -- A collection of maps.

Bibliographic Information -- Information that identifies a work including title, author, publisher, and date of publication. Bibliographic information on an item is called a citation.

Bibliography -- A list of citations to materials such as books, articles, reports, videos, and Internet sites on a subject. Bibliographies are usually arranged in alphabetical order. Research papers and books usually have a bibliography of materials used to create that work.

Biography -- Information about a person's life. An autobiography is a biography written by that same person.

Book Catalog -- A list or printout in book form of materials such as books, periodicals, reports, and videos found in a library.

Boolean Operators -- Words used to connect two or more concepts/subject terms. AND will combine two concepts/subject terms to create one concept. OR will allow the user to locate synonyms or like terms. NOT excludes a term from a search.

Bound Periodicals -- Back issues of magazines and journals. The term "bound" implies paper copies, although back issues can also be stored on microforms and in electronic formats like CD-ROM.

Call Number -- A special code or "address" that is given to a book or other piece of material in a library to indicates its location. A system of call numbers is called a classification system.

Card Catalog -- A listing in card form of the holdings of a library. A card catalog can be divided into subject, title, and author segments or combined into one big "dictionary" type.

Catalog -- A listing of materials owned by a library. They can be found in book, card, sheaf, or electronic formats.

CD-ROM -- Compact Disk-Read Only Memory (CD-ROM) is the storage of information on a small circular disk. Many things (music, videos, etc.) are stored on CD-ROMs, including searchable databases of information.

Circulating Book -- A book that can be checked out from the library. Some library materials, such as periodicals or reference books, do not circulate.

Citation -- The necessary information for locating each item in a database. A citation usually includes the author, title, publication information, and date of publication. A list of citations on a subject is called a bibliography.

Classification System -- A system for organizing library materials. Major classification systems in libraries include Library of Congress, Dewey Decimal and the Superintendent of Documents.

Controlled Vocabulary -- Subject headings used in a specific index or database. Subject headings used in one index are not necessarily the same as those used in another.

Cross Reference -- A reference (in a catalog or index) that steers the user to more information or to other search terms for a particular subject.

Dictionary -- A work that gives definitions of words. Each entry may also indicate different spellings, pronunciations, usage and/or syllabication.

Descriptors -- Another word for subject headings.

Download -- Transferring information in electronic format to a floppy disk.

Electronic Database -- A file or collection of records in machine-readable format. Online catalogs and periodical indexes are electronic databases.

Fields -- The segments of a citation such as author, title, and subject. The term "fields" is usually associated with electronic databases.

Field Searching -- Most electronic databases allow the user to search for information by specific field. Searching for "Martin Luther King, Jr." in the subject field will return records *about* him. Searching in the author field will return records to materials written *by* him.

Gazetteer -- A place-name dictionary. Use it to look up information about a geographic place, such as Sahara Desert or Argentina. A gazetteer may only provide the location of a place or may also give other information about the place.

Government Publications -- Information published by or at the expense of a government agency. Many publications are required by law or are necessary for an agency to accomplish its mission.

Holdings -- The books, periodicals, and other materials in a library's possession. A library may subscribe to a magazine but may have possession of only a few years' worth of issues. The "holdings statement" will specify exactly which issues the library owns.

HTTP -- HyperText Transfer Protocol.

Hypertext -- Text in Internet documents which link to other documents, whether text, pictures, or sound. Such cross-referernces make it possible to follow information in a non-linear fashion, by jumping from document to document as needed.

Imprint -- A statement that includes all of the publishing information for a work, such as place of publication, publisher and year of publication.

Index -- A systematic guide to locating items or information (journal articles, books, newspaper articles) by author, title and subject, usually in alphabetical order. The format can be paper, microform or electronic.

Inverted Heading -- A subject heading that has the most important word placed first. Such as *Missouri, University of.*

Internet -- A worldwide network of computers connected together with communication cables.

Journal -- A periodical publication that normally published by a recognized professional organization for people who are familiar with the subject content.

Library of Congress Subject Headings -- Four volume set of books containing subject headings/controlled vocabulary and cross references used in a library's online catalog.

Magazine -- A general-subject periodical publication produced for commercial distribution such as *Time, Newsweek, Redbook,* and *Business Week.* Magazines cover many subjects and are written for the lay person.

Manuscript -- Original papers (often thought of as being handwritten) produced by a person at the time of a particular event. A diary is a manuscript, as are letters and first drafts of books.

Microform -- Material reproduced in smaller size, usually placed on transparent medium such as microfilm and microfiche, requiring a machine to read it.

Online Catalog -- An electronic index to the holdings of a library.

Periodical -- Any publication that is issued on a regular basis -- magazines, journals, newspapers, yearbooks, almanacs, and encyclopedias.

Prefatory Pages -- Pages in the front of a paper index that explain how to use it.

Record -- Collection of fields containing information about a particular item such as a book, journal, or magazine article, located in an index or database.

Reference Book -- A book which contains a lot of information about a topic. It is not something one reads straight through, but uses to look up pieces of information.

Search Strategy -- The planned process that one uses to locate information. Selection of the index/database is probably the first step. In using an electronic database, the search strategy is the information that you type into the computer in order to retrieve the records on that subject.

Sheaf Catalog -- A loose-leaf notebook listing of library materials.

Subject Heading -- Word(s) indicating a subject under which all material dealing with that subject is entered.

SUDOC Number -- The call number system (Superintendent of Documents) for Government Documents.

Thesaurus -- Another name for a subject heading guide to an index or database. A thesaurus is also a book of synonyms compiled to aid writers.

Truncation -- The ability to search using fragments of words in order to broaden the search strategy.

Unabridged Dictionary -- Comprehensive dictionaries containing more than 250,000 words.

Yearbook -- A book published every year. Yearbooks are often updating tools for a preexisting work, such as an encyclopedia.

WAIS -- (Wide Area Information System) Allows searching of information by key concept, or within full text, across various Internet hosts.

World Wide Web -- A computerized body of information stored on computers around the world. The information is organized and linked by hypertext and accessed using the Internet.

Index

Subject Headings in Bold Type

Subject Headings in Bold Type

Subject Headings in Bold Type

Subject Headings in Bold Type

Subject Headings in Bold Type

Subject Headings in Bold Type

Subject Headings in Bold Type